KU-454-750

Management and Delivery of Social Care

by

Max Taylor

and

Christine Vigars

LONGMAN

Published by Longman Information and Reference,
Longman Group UK Ltd, 6th Floor, Westgate House, The High,
Harlow, Essex CM20 1YR, England and Associated Companies
throughout the world.

© Longman Group UK Ltd 1993

All rights reserved. No part of this publication may be reproduced, stored in a retrieval
system, or transmitted in any form or by any means, electronic, mechanical,
photocopying, recording or otherwise, without the prior permission of the Copyright
owner or a licence permitting restricted copying issued by the Copyright Licensing
Agency Ltd., 90 Tottenham Court Road, London W1P 9HE.

A catalogue record for this book is available from The British Library

ISBN 0-582-20962-5

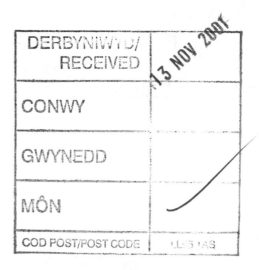

DERBYNIWYD/
RECEIVED   13 NOV 2001

CONWY

GWYNEDD

MÔN

COD POST/POST CODE   LL55 1AS

Typeset by Anglia Photoset Ltd,
34A St Botolph's Church Walk, St Botolph's Street,
Colchester, Essex CO2 7EA.

Printed in Great Britain by BPCC Wheatons Ltd, Exeter

Contents

Acknowledgements

We wish to thank the following for case-study material included in chapter 9:

Jim Armstrong and Russ Kanger of The Adolescents and Children Trust

Susan Dunn and Alan Grierson of Opportunities and Networks in Southwark

Keith Smith of Lewisham Social Services

Introduction: aims and themes

The aim of this book is to help people manage social work better, particularly in the light of changes implied by the Children Act 1989, and the National Health Service and Community Care Act 1990. The book should help individual social workers in managing cases; it should also help social work managers, in assembling packages of care and assessing quality, and in getting the best performance from their own staff. Finally it should help independent providers of services, in giving the level of service required, and managing their schemes. Most of the book applies to all three kinds of reader (more specialised sections will be obvious from their headings).

The book has a number of central arguments.

1. Front-line workers in social work are more and more required to act in a way that is essentially managerial. Three new factors have led to this:

- The development of care management;
- The growth of community care, which involves encouraging community development and supporting small voluntary groups:
- The split between contractors and suppliers, which involves the need both to encourage and control private suppliers. Management opportunities will also expand through the growth of small autonomous units.

2. For a service organisation in a changing context, the right management style is participative rather than autocratic. This is particularly needed when large, bureaucratic organisations are likely to be replaced by smaller ones based on flexible teams.

3. Good management is not so much a matter of strategic thinking as of effective behaviour. Behaviour depends largely on skills, and all skills can be learnt. Alike among managers, workers and clients, the potential for improvement is vast.

4. Attention to management behaviour can improve the delivery of services in the public sector — but at the same time it is important to recognise differences between public and private sectors.

5. Partnership with clients means extending to them the same sort of participation that a good manager offers her staff, and needs the same attitudes and skills.

6. Community care as a way of working depends on skills of community social work, such as developing networks, and working in partnership with voluntary groups.

7. Principles of equality should underlie both the management and the delivery of social services.

8. The new legislation can only work to the benefit of social services, if the change is handled right on the ground: and the new skills — of specifying and monitoring the quality of services, working at second hand through independent units, and managing in a more flexible way — are widely developed among social service staff.

1 The new world of social work

1.1 The rival philosophies

1993 was a year of quiet revolution in social work in Britain. Throughout the 1980s two rival philosophies struggled for dominance across large tracts of government and public service: the Old Left–Centre philosophy of public provision and the New Right doctrine of the free market. Social Services, however, were largely unaffected by these traumas, except for a slower growth of funds. There was new legislation at the end of the eighties — the Children Act 1989 and the NHS and Community Care Act 1990, but it was only in 1993 that the changes they brought in began to have a major impact on the lives of social workers, and the provision of social care. Some social workers felt that the changes undermined values they cherished, and threatened the well-being of clients: others welcomed the market culture, as holding out the prospect of more autonomy for workers, and better service for clients (as authors, we started on opposite sides of the debate and only came in time to the shared statement in the introduction).

The new Acts, and other legislation such as the Criminal Justice Act, will have a revolutionary impact on social work management, and cause many changes in methods of delivery. To understand the effects, it is necessary to look first at the rival philosophies, and see what the changes were designed to achieve.

The values of the Old Left–Centre, which go back to the origins of the welfare state, can be summarised as follows:

— A system of state welfare which provides for those in need, through unemployment, poverty, illness, or other incapacity
— Collective responsibility
— Universal entitlement to benefits, paid for through a combination of taxation and insurance
— Services subject to political accountability through local democracy
— An ethos of public service, with an emphasis on justice, equity and citizenship
— An image of welfare professionals as being at the heart of public service.

By contrast, the doctrines of the New Right are based on the following premises:

— State provision should be targeted on those who are most in need
— Market mechanisms and competition should be used wherever possible to provide a spur to efficiency
— Local authority monopolies of provision should be broken up
— Competition will provide greater individual choice
— Management concepts and practices from the private sector will increase efficiency in the public sector
— Costs must be controlled by greater efficiency

The emphasis put on competition can be expanded. The assumption is not simply that competition makes people work harder — where ideals are strong, as in social work, this may not be so. Rather in a more diverse world there is room for a variety of methods and approaches, and those that work best will tend to thrive and spread. There is also a change in the balance of risk. In a traditional bureaucracy, there is not much incentive to back new ideas: they may succeed or they may fail, and the penalties of failure loom far larger than the rewards of success. In a competitive market, the rewards of being first with a good idea are very great, so there is constant pressure towards innovation.

Though these beliefs are credited to the 'new Right', there is not necessarily anything anti-egalitarian about them. One could hold these beliefs and still feel that a great deal more should be done to help the poor — indeed some Labour councils have been among the pioneers in using market-based systems (though not yet in social work). However (the Old Left might say) in a competitive system, although there may be some excellent schemes, there will be many dishonest, profiteering and slothful ones. Only the most rigorous inspection can make sure that private suppliers do not take advantage of public funds and uncomplaining customers. At least the aim of bureaucracy — if not always its effect in practice — was to provide equal services for equal needs.

In one sense this argument is academic: what matters in the real world is not who wins the intellectual argument, but who won the last election. The new methods are coming in, and will be with us for the foreseeable future, and it is in the interests both of clients and staff that they should work well. Some parallel developments in other parts of the public sector are the introduction of compulsory competitive tendering for council services, local management of schools (following the Education Reform Act 1988), the reduction of the role of local authorities in housing (Housing Act 1988), and within the NHS, the introduction of general managers, the purchaser/provider split, and the internal market. All these measures are aimed at controlling costs, while at the same time increasing users' choice. One of the arguments between the two philosophies is on whether these two objectives are compatible, or diametrically opposed. The dispute has been aggravated by the slower growth of social service funds overall, and the cutbacks in those authorities that are subject to capping. Workers in many authorities are left wondering how far re-organisation is a rational response to new policy, and how far it is simply a cost-cutting exercise.

1.2 The new legislation

Over the last three years, the legal framework of social work has been changed by three major pieces of legislation: the Children Act 1989, the NHS and Community Care Act 1990, and the Criminal Justice Act 1991.

The *Children Act* sets out a new framework both for public and private law. Its central belief is that children are best looked after in families, and that parents should be encouraged to exercise the responsibilities as well as the rights of parenthood. Social Services are expected to work with families to support them and prevent the need for intervention through the courts. Among its main provisions are:

— A statement that the welfare of the child is paramount
— A new concept of parental responsibility
— Emphasis on partnership with parents in the provision of services

— A requirement that local authorities must identify children in need and provide services for their families
— A principle of minimal intervention and a presumption that no order will be made
— A clear distinction between children who are accommodated at the request of parents, and those subject to an order
— A requirement that in providing services for children, local authorities must take account of their racial, cultural, linguistic and religious backgrounds.

The Children Act concentrates on the welfare of the child but the *Criminal Justice Act* moves away from considering the 'welfare' of the offender in decisions on sentencing. The Act arises from debates in the 1980s between a 'welfare' approach to juvenile offenders which looked for reasons for crime in the background of the offender and a 'justice' approach which concentrated on the circumstances and nature of the offence. Proponents of the justice approach argued that the discussion of personal and family background in social enquiry reports paradoxically led to sentences for young people being *more* severe than their offences warranted. The 1991 Act supports this view, by introducing a framework which links the severity of the sentence to the severity of the offence. It introduces threshold criteria for bringing cases to court and for progression through the available sentences. Pre-sentence reports are written to a format which considers the seriousness of the offence and mitigating circumstances, and offers a proposal for the guidance of the court. The Act is based on the principle of minimum intervention consistent with the seriousness of the offence, and strongly encourages diversion from prosecution through police cautioning.

The *NHS and Community Care Act* has re-organised services for adults who need support because of ageing, mental illness, physical disabilities, learning difficulties, or drug and alcohol dependence. Throughout the 1980s the population of elderly people, especially those over eighty, expanded rapidly, and there were more and more people living in their own homes who needed care. At the same time it was decided to close down the large hospitals for people with learning difficulties, while changes in the treatment of the mentally ill led to the emptying of psychiatric hospitals. Government expenditure on care of the elderly continued to rise, and an Audit Commission report of 1986[1] pointed out the perverse incentive of paying for private residential care through the social security budget.

The main proposals of the Act are based on the 1989 White Paper *Caring for People*,[2] which sets out six main objectives:

— Enabling people to live in their own homes, with the support of community services

- Providing practical support for carers
- Introducing assessment and care management
- Encouraging the provision of services by the independent sector
- Making social services more accountable
- Ensuring value for money

These objectives are to be achieved by the transfer of funds from the national Social Security budget to local Social Services departments, which become the lead agencies for community care. Within the local authority, the Act implies a separation between the functions of purchasing and providing services, in a manner similar to the internal market in the National Health Service. The Act doesn't simply re-organise services for particular client groups, but requires changes in both the structure of services, and social work practice. The main changes are:

- Local authorities will buy-in services from suppliers: in-house suppliers must compete with the independent sector for contracts
- Quality control, through service specifications and monitoring of contract compliance
- Registration and inspection of homes by arms-length inspection units
- Agencies must agree on a systematic approach to the assessment of need
- Defining criteria for eligibility
- Preparation of individual care plans (for complex cases)
- Setting up a complaints procedure

The Children Act and the NHS and Community Care Act have important themes in common, including:

- the principles of partnership, empowerment and user choice
- an emphasis on needs-led assessment
- care plans for individuals.

The NHS and Community Care Act also introduces a split between the role of purchasing care services, and the role of providing them: although this is only mandatory for adults, a number of authorities are introducing it for children's services as well.

1.3 Problems of implementation

The working of all three Acts is still controversial (Summer 1993).

There is concern that the policy changes may have been taken too far, and doubt whether Local Authorities can implement the legislation at a time when resources are being cut back. The first year of implementation of the Children Act saw a dramatic fall in the number of applications to court, and court orders: exact comparisons are difficult, but it seems that both emergency protection orders and care orders halved over the year to October 1992, while the numbers of children on the child protection register fell by 15 per cent in the six months to March 1992. The principle of minimal intervention is obviously working, but there is concern that social services departments may now be too reluctant to seek court orders, even when this would clearly be in the interests of the child. The Social Services Inspectorate comment that working in partnership should not dissuade Social Services from seeking court orders as part of a planned process.[3] The number of young people appearing in the Youth Courts has shown a similar decline, though it is too soon to say whether this is due to more use of police cautioning. Meanwhile public debate is raging about the extent of juvenile crime: Home Office statistics show a substantial fall, both in the number of known juvenile offenders and the number of prosecutions. These figures have been greeted with disbelief, and the government has responded with proposals to re-introduce secure schools, and increase the number of secure places in local authority care. There is similar public concern about moving psychiatric patients into the community, and the Minister of Health has announced a review of the Mental Health Act 1983 to consider introducing 'supervised discharge', which would ensure that psychiatric patients take their medication. Moreover the formal assessment of need will show up many grave problems that were previously unidentified, with little prospect of funds to meet them (see chapter 3).

The other main concern is whether implementation can be adequately resourced. A survey in January 1993 by the Association of Directors of Social Services showed that 80 per cent of members were expecting budget cuts, coinciding with the implementation of community care.[4] The amount of funds transferred to local authorities from the social security budget is tied to the provision of independent residential care: in other words, there is still a bias towards residential care, and this may well inhibit the development of domiciliary care. The survival of drug and alcohol projects is threatened, since their specific grant is now to be incorporated into the community care budget. The government grant for AIDs and HIV work is threatened, as is 'Section 11' funding for work with ethnic minorities. The effects of the drive to reduce public expenditure are most acute in those authorities faced with capping, many of whom are in inner cities with high levels of social need. In these circumstances it is hard to see how the Acts can be successfully implemented. The Review of the first year of the Children Act shows that seventeen authorities had more than 20 children on the Child Protection Register still unallocated to homes, while fourteen had more than 30 children who are being 'looked after', still unallocated.[5] It is obvious that in these authorities, children are not getting adequate care or protection. The cuts fall heaviest on independent local schemes like family centres, which do most to help families stay together, and whose survival is crucial if there is to be a thriving voluntary sector in community care.

1.4   The demand for management

The philosophy of the New Right brings with it a requirement for changes in the way government is run. Traditionally the public and private sectors have been run in very different ways. The private sector strove for good management, the public sector for sound administration. According to Sir Roy Griffiths[6] the administrative model involves working within a hierarchical structure, following set rules and procedures which stifle innovation and initiative. This is not to say that private industry cannot be bureaucratic too, but it is restrained by the discipline of the market: given competition, less effective firms tend to shrink, while more effective ones grow. By contrast, the size of government departments is not determined by their success — indeed if a department fails to deliver, the natural response in a bureaucracy is to give it more resources, so reinforcing failure. Some special problems of local government are:

1. Committees of elected members may be the best people to decide what the public wants done, but they are not so good at deciding *how* things should be done. A large committee of non-specialists is likely to be both slower and more erratic than a small group of professionals.
2. Senior officers spend time managing political committees, which absorbs more time and energy than reporting to a Board of Directors.
3. The need to safeguard public funds involves bureaucratic checks and slows the response.
4. Annual budget-setting is dependent on the level of government funding, which makes long term planning difficult.
5. The legislation requires comprehensive coverage; expensive services for vulnerable groups of people can't simply be cut.

Since the Seebohm report, social services have been one of the biggest local authority departments, in terms both of staffing and expenditure. The director has been a powerful figure among chief officers, while the chair of the social services committee has been a prize for local politicians. There have been tensions about the respective roles of officers and members, while inside the department there has been a long-running debate about the status of the profession within a bureaucracy, the professionals trying to preserve their independence from political interference or management control.

Under the new system, a great deal of work will be transferred from the public to the private sector, where private sector methods will presumably prevail. However even within the public sector a new emphasis on management will be needed to cope with the new systems. It is a key belief of the new public management[7] that political policy-making should be separate and distinct from management. Managers should:

— Have the freedom to manage
— Ensure cost effectiveness
— Base their approach on setting performance targets and monitoring output.
— Encourage competition and contracting out
— Introduce monetary incentives.

Obviously this won't solve all the problems. There is nothing here to overcome the problems of central government funding (though private firms are dependent on cash flow, which can be just as erratic). To work at all, the new style will have to start at the top — Committees and Councillors will have to accept a changed role, setting policies but leaving managers to manage. If they do however, if budgets are devolved and directors operate through monitoring performance, public sector managers will be much more in the position of private sector ones, being judged on results rather than on conformity to procedures. There are important implications for the way teams and units are run, and these are some of the main themes of the book.

To respond to the new demands, the large bureaucratic structures are being broken up, and powers and budgets being delegated to smaller units. Social Services departments are now being divided into four functions — Purchasing, Provision, Support services, and Policy.[8] These are discussed below:

1. Purchasing. There can be a conflict between economies of scale and allowing users more choice. Most authorities will have a central commissioning and contracting unit, perhaps shared with the Health Service, to negotiate block contracts with major suppliers. However some purchasing powers may be devolved to the service units responsible for assessment and care management, which will give them a chance to meet the special needs of clients and of their locality, and to offer more choice.

2. *Provision.* In-house providers are likely to be hived off as business units, tendering in competition with outside providers. In time this may lead to a reduction in the direct provision of services. The outside providers may be part of a large voluntary organisation, or be small independent units; in either case they will control their own budgets and set their own priorities.

3. *Support services.* As power is devolved to local units, they may well press for the right to buy services such as transport and training from outside the Department. A decision has to be taken on which services will still be provided centrally, either for reasons of quality control, or to secure economies of scale.

4. *Policy.* Responsibility for policy remains squarely with local councillors, advised by the senior officers. However the line between policy and implementation is never hard and fast, and if need is to be assessed at local level, local decisions may be better at meeting it. Some authorities with devolved structures have already introduced local posts for policy and development, and a similar management structure for provider units.

Small independent units will need all the processes of management — staff, purchasing, selling and policy making. As such units become more common, there will be a corresponding growth in the number of people involved in management. At the same time redefining the task of social work will call for more management skills within local authorities themselves. There will be greater demands on senior staff, and a dramatic widening of management opportunities.

1.5 Changes in social work practice

(a) Community care and case management

The Acts reinforce some changes that were already happening for other reasons, but also introduce a need for some quite new skills. During the 1970s and 1980s, the large long-stay hospitals were closed, and the main job of community care was re-establishing their patients in community settings. This also became a focus of research: some of the earliest work took place in Kent, Gateshead and

Darlington, and led to the development of a model scheme of case management for the support of the frail elderly in the community. In 1983, a number of pilot projects were set up and evaluated by the Personal Social Services Research Unit of Kent University,[9] covering various client groups — the elderly, and people with learning difficulties, mental health problems, and physical disabilities. Case management aims to give clients long-term support, rather than therapy or solving short-term problems: it fills a gap identified in the social work literature, and will help to redress the neglect these client groups have suffered in the community.

The model has wider organisational implications. The demonstration projects set up in 1983 were required by the Department of Health to be inter-agency, and this led to various forms of multi-disciplinary working, both between health and social services, and between the statutory and voluntary sectors. Assistants or para-professionals were used in case management, so challenging the received views about the role of professionals. In Kent, case managers were given their own budgets, which allowed them flexibility in purchasing services. In this they were the precursors of the new legislation.

So far the new processes of assessment and care management were based on the old skills of social care planning, as established in community social work:

— mobilising existing networks
— extending and developing new ones
— liaising and negotiating with community groups
— identifying unmet needs
— working in partnership with families
— acting as advocate, in dealings with official bodies.

They required strong skills of team-work (often in multi-disciplinary groups) and the ability to work across professional boundaries. However, delegation of budgets, to the first line manager or even the individual worker, requires a new set of skills:

— working within a budget
— negotiating with suppliers
— setting standards
— monitoring the quality of service delivery.

(b) Choice, empowerment and partnership

These skills reflect a shift in the traditional understanding of 'good practice'. Traditional values were concerned with client self-determination, but in community care the new emphasis is on customer choice. In practice there may be less choice, because of block purchasing and the need to ration resources — or what choice there is may be exercised by the care manager rather than the client. The main ways in which choice can be extended are (i) in residential and day care in the details of daily life, and (ii) by social workers making plans *with* people rather than for them.

Sometimes of course, where the client is involuntary and social work is concerned with surveillance rather than service, there is no choice at all. The same argument applies in the shift from 'enablement' to 'empowerment'. Helping clients to help themselves has long been an aim of case work, self-help groups and community development, and offering a choice of services certainly gives clients more power to decide their own future. But in surveillance cases, once again there is no real scope for power sharing: the social worker or the court has taken charge, and though they can consult, they cannot devolve the essential decisions. It is however possible to make sure that the professional's actions are monitored, to give clients more information, and to help them gain strength through links with other people.

In the same way, 'agreement' on case-work goals is meant to be replaced by 'partnership'. Partnership normally means working together for mutual benefit, which is not really the case in social work, since the client is the beneficiary (though the social worker gets paid). But social worker and client can certainly work together — even in surveillance cases where it is the client's self-control that may be the focus of attention — and people can be consulted and involved far more than they are at present.

These values of choice, partnership and empowerment are linked to a concern for equal opportunities, and can be derived from the traditional values of autonomy and respect for persons. They imply a culture within social services of giving free access to information, allowing parents and users to take part in case conferences, and offering a ready procedure for dealing with complaints. Below are two examples of this new approach:

1. **Mrs Henry** is a 80-year-old Irishwoman, cared for by her adult daughter, who has reached the point of approaching Social Services for help. Under the old system, Mrs Henry would have been assessed for Part 3 by the adviser for the elderly, and her case would have been put to a panel, to decide whether she met the priority categories for allocation to the next vacancy in a local authority home. She would then be told the result. The assessment would therefore be service-led, giving power to the adviser rather than the client.

A needs-led assessment puts Mrs Henry at the centre of the process, and considers her wishes as well as the pressures on her carer. The available options are: provision of respite care; a place in private residential care; or a care package designed to relieve the daughter, drawing on voluntary sources such as a pensioners' visiting scheme or day centre. The assessment will take account of Mrs Henry's cultural and religious needs and her view of the ageing process. The options would be discussed with both of them, and the choice made jointly.

2. **Mr and Mrs Yates** are a white couple who have a son aged 14 with learning difficulties. Because an older sister died young in suspicious circumstances, the son has been on a supervision order since birth. This order ensures that a social worker undertakes periodic reviews, but little other work has been done. Mr and Mrs Yates have become quite used to social work oversight, but have never had the chance to question it.

With the coming into force of the Children Act, an assessment was required to see what order if any was appropriate, the main considerations being the welfare and protection of the child. Following the assessment, goals were set, in partnership with the parents, to extend the boy's social networks. Mr and Mrs Yates' parenting skills were assessed and reinforced, and they were referred to a parents' group for help in overcoming the delayed shock and grief caused by the original death. A recommendation was made that the supervision order should lapse.

1.6 Equal opportunities and anti-discriminatory practice

All employers are forbidden by law to discriminate on grounds of race or sex, but social service departments are in a special position which makes the avoidance of discrimination a cornerstone of their policy. Their work is mostly among the poor, and in this country many of the poorest people come from black and ethnic minority communities, and to date, social services have not done much to improve their lot. Social workers need to understand the unequal take-up of services and the pervasive nature of racism, and to develop ways of working which are sensitive to the needs of black people. However minority communities are not well represented among social workers, and hardly at all in social work management. This means that an important target of policy should be the recruitment of black professionals. The aim is not that all clients should be able to deal with a social worker from their own ethnic group — this would not be practical and might not be desirable: what is essential is that social workers should have regular professional contact with colleagues who belong to the same ethnic groups as their customers.

The legal framework is set out by the Equal Pay Act 1970, the Sex Discrimination Act 1975, and the Race Relations Act 1976. The Sex Discrimination Act applies both to men and women and covers recruitment, training, promotion and dismissal. The Race Relations Act 1976 (Section 71) imposes a duty on all local authorities to eliminate unlawful discrimination, and promote equality of opportunity and good relations between people of different racial groups. This applies to all the authority's services and employment practices. Within this framework, the Children Act (and related regulations and guidance) imposes a duty on local authorities, both in providing day care and in recruiting foster carers, to consider the racial groups to which children in need belong. Section 22, which applies to placement in substitute family care and to children's homes, says that due consideration must be given to a child's 'religious persuasion, racial origin and cultural and linguistic background'. The Department of Health circular *Principles and Practice in Regulations and Guidance*[10] considers 'institutional racism' in the provision of services, and emphasises work with extended families, consultation with black community groups, and the need in work with children to help them to develop a positive self-image, and regard for their own ethnic and cultural origins. The Criminal Justice Act 1991 (section 95) places a duty on the Secretary of State to monitor against improper discrimination, and the Home Office have issued guidance on setting standards for non-discriminatory language in pre-sentence reports.[11]

The White paper *Caring for People — Community Care in the next decade and beyond* recognised that people from different backgrounds may have particular care needs, and that minority communities may have different concepts of community care, and stressed the need to consult minority community groups. The Community Care Act chose not to enforce this recommendation, but it is clearly in line with its spirit, as is the need for services to reflect the diversity of cultural need and racial origin. Black-run projects can therefore be encouraged to tender to provide services, and service providers can be monitored to see that they avoid discrimination.

Since 1971, the social services work-force has contained a predominance of women at lower grades, and a concentration of black women in the post of care assistant, and in domestic and ancillary jobs in residential homes. Managers above the level of team leader are predominantly men, while women Directors of Social Services are very rare indeed. Because family and caring are thought of as women's work, it is mostly women who approach Social Services for help and, since the need for services is linked to poverty, predominantly working class women. One serious concern

about the current shift into community care is that it will increase
the financial and emotional strain on women carers. As women live
longer than men, there are more older women than men in need of
day and residential care. The residential needs of Lesbian women
and gay men are generally ignored by social services (except in
services for people who have Aids or are HIV positive).

Many studies have shown that black and ethnic minority users
and workers continue to suffer discrimination. In 1978 the Association of Directors of Social Services described the responses of their
Departments to a multiracial society as 'patchy, piecemeal and
lacking in strategy'.[12] A 1988 report of the Social Services Inspectorate noted that a majority of the 24 departments visited had no policy
for responding to the needs of a multiracial population.[13] The 1992
report on the first year of the implementation of the Children Act
shows that only 60 out of 108 Local Authorities had publicised their
services in languages other than English.

The requirements of the new legislation will be set within the
local framework of an equal opportunities policy. In the Race
Equality Unit publication *Equally Fair*,[14] some key components of
this are listed. The department should publish a policy statement
dealing with the delivery of services. It should state aims and
objectives in relation to race equality, include a strategy for implementation, and say who is responsible. The department should also
monitor the delivery of all its services, through a system of ethnic
records. (This approach could be extended to other disadvantaged
groups.) Using these criteria, the REU study found that 60 per cent
of the departments studied had made little or no progress in
developing equal opportunities policies. The authors conclude that
'It appears that in the great majority of social services departments,
the equal opportunities service delivery policy and monitoring
framework needs to be developed'. The study links the lack of
progress to the historical dominance of ideas like 'colour blindness'
or 'cultural diversity' rather than 'anti-racism'. Departments have
either claimed to treat all users the same regardless of race or culture,
or have concentrated on cultural diversity without recognising the
impact of discrimination. Such approaches are no longer in line with
government policy.

It is important to recognise that no Social Services department in
England and Wales is without an ethnic minority population, often
concentrated in small areas within predominantly white communities, and that issues such as ethnic record-keeping apply to all of
them. Without corrective policies, black clients will continue to be
channelled into the controlling aspects of social work, such as
prisons, psychiatric hospitals, and child protection registers, and
be denied access to therapeutic or supportive services. Black workers

will continue to be seen as 'race experts' — be overloaded with
ethnic minority clients, asked to act as interpreters, or expected to
take the initiative in confronting discriminatory practices. A policy
framework is essential, but its implementation to make sure that
such practices are altered is a job of management.

1.7 Management and mystique

Management means leading a team that gets things done. This
involves setting objectives, and adjusting them when the world
changes. It also includes organising workers into an effective team,
and motivating, developing and pushing them to get results. As a
rule, people work best if they are led in a participative way — both
because they will be better motivated, and because if they are
encouraged to speak their minds, they will produce valuable ideas
and essential information. However no one style works in every
situation, and there are times when good managers have to close
down discussion and drive towards action.

The work managers do is a balance between aiming towards
long-term goals, and keeping alert to deal with the here and now. Of
the two, here and now is often more important: in industry, if you
set the wrong goals you may go bust next year, but if you fail to
respond to the current crisis, you could go bust tomorrow. Management involves dealing effectively with a series of problems, most
fairly minor, and not many of them intellectually demanding. What
is difficult is taking in a huge mass of data, spotting what is really
serious, sorting it out and switching quickly to something different.

The qualities of a good manager are very like those of a good
social worker. This is not surprising, since their jobs have a large
element in common — getting other people to behave in a sensible
and co-operative way. Social workers may see themselves as kind-
hearted and concerned, whereas managers are tough: however
managers who are any good are very much concerned with the
welfare of their staff, while social workes need a degree of detach-
ment. Indeed one problem of the new contractual system is that
social service staff, in an attempt to be 'managerial', may be driving
too hard a bargain (see chapter 3).

Although there are dozens of management theories, there is no
grand Theory of Management. Management draws on many different disciplines — psychology (for human relations and marketing),
economics, statistics, computing, law, and accountancy. Most of
management learning consists of devices for tackling recurrent

business problems — motivating staff, costing capital expenditure, or developing new products. Management pundits tend to come up with a simple, sensible idea which they then broaden and complicate for all it is worth — partly because the owners of ideas love them dearly, partly because the greater the complexity, the more scope there is for acting as a consultant or writing books. This is one main cause of the mystique of management. Because management deals with such a variety of cases, no management idea is universally helpful. Take, for example, a sound and simple idea such as 'management by objectives'. If you, as a manager, agree objectives with your team members, this will help to motivate them, channel their efforts in the right direction, and make your job of leadership and supervision easier. However if staff get so wrapped up in pursuing their objectives that they neglect the more mundane parts of their job, disaster can follow. Every management idea must be used in moderation, and with sense.

One of the themes of this book is that success or failure depends not so much on right policy — let alone management theory — but on management *behaviour*. When management pundits write up case studies, they tend to concentrate on the strategic decisions — for example, the failure to foresee that one product was obsolescent, and another about to take over. What they tend to ignore is that bad strategic decisions don't happen out of the blue — they are made by people who are not doing their jobs. Underlying any management disaster, there is a failure of behaviour: managers were too arrogant to listen, too lazy to read their papers, too cowardly to take risks, or too unskilled to create an organisation in which staff could speak up.

Most often the failure is one of skill. The skills managers need are of three sorts:

- Professional skills. For social work managers, this means not just dealing with clients, but commissioning, inspecting, handling budgets and (looked at from the providers' point of view) marketing, and selling.
- Human skills — listening, persuading, leading, supervising, motivating and many others.
- Skills of getting things done. Particularly aim-setting, finding information, planning, getting into action, and reviewing.

In this book, these last skills are dealt with first (in chapter 2), because they underlie the others (it requires *planning* to deal with staff, carry out professional work, sell your products etc.). The procedures may seem basic, but they are what matters. What managers need most is not sophisticated theory, but a thorough understanding of some rather simple practices which underlie management at all levels. In chapters 3 to 5 the book goes on to look at the new (or newly important) processes of assessing needs and commissioning, budgeting and monitoring services. Chapter 6 deals with the skills of handling staff and dealing with people: chapter 7 applies the same principles to dealings outside the department — to networking, and co-operating with other bodies. Chapter 8 deals with development and self-development, and chapter 9 with the management of change.

Notes

1   Audit Commission (1986) *Making a Reality of Community Care*. London: HMSO.
2   Department of Health (1989) *Caring for People: Community Care in the next decade and beyond*. London: HMSO.
3   Department of Health (1992) *Children Act Report 1992*. London: HMSO.
4   NACRO/Department of Health (1992) *Criminal Justice Act 1991*. Training Pack.
5   *Community Care* April 1, 1993 p. 3.
6   Griffiths, R. (1992) 'With the past behind us' *Community Care* January 16 pp. 18–21.
7   On the new public management see: Hood, C. (1991) 'A public management for all seasons?' *Public Administration* Spring **69** pp. 3–19. Hunter, D. (1993) 'To market! To market! A new dawn for community care'. *Health and Social Care in the Community* Vol. 1 No. 1 January pp. 3–10.
8   Flynn, N. (1990) *Public Sector Management*.
9   Knapp, M., Cambridge, P., Thomason, C., Beacham, J., Allen, C., Darton, R. (1992) *Care in the Community; Challenge and Demonstration*.
10 Department of Health (1989) *Principles and Practice in Regulations and Guidance*.
11 See 'Gender and pre-sentence reports' and 'Race and pre-sentence reports' in NACRO pack, as above.
12 ADSS/CRE (1976) *Multi-racial Britain: the Social Services response*.
13 CRE (1989) *Racial Equality in Social Services Departments: a survey of equal opportunity policies*.
14 Butt, J., Gorbach, P., Ahmad, B. (1991) *Equally Fair?* (Race Equality Unit/NISW/Social Service Research Group).

2 Aims, targets and getting results

Social work — like architecture and engineering, but unlike law and accountancy — is an achieving profession: its function is getting things done. All kinds of active work have three basic stages in common:

1. Establishing what is wanted, and why
2. Organising the actions that will achieve it
3. Reviewing, to check whether the job is complete, and to learn from the experience.

These three stages have themselves been codified, to form a sort of ABC of getting things done. If we don't usually think in these terms, it reflects one of the faults of our education system, which teaches us how to think but not how to act. A formula like this is not much help in routine activities, when you know what you are trying to do, and how to set about it. It comes into its own when work is complex or unfamiliar, and in managing or co-operating with other people. It is therefore a good starting point for looking at management in a changing environment.

2.1 Getting things done

Task-centred practice

Many social workers will be familiar with Task Centred Practice — a way of working with clients through encouraging them to tackle their own problems, with the support and collaboration of their worker. It is a useful approach to social work, though obviously not the only one. What matters here is the working sequence that has been defined for it (by Doel and Marsh, 1992), whose stages are shown in Fig. 2.1.[1]

Establish mandate for work (purpose of intervention etc.)

Explore problems
    Select and agree on problem
    Establish tasks ('series of steps within overall plan')

Task implementation
    Enhance commitment
    Plan task implementation
    Analyse obstacles
    Model, rehearse and use guided practice
    Summarise plan for action

Action

Review

Figure 2.1

This sequence is very similar to procedures that have been designed for quite different purposes — for example, the 'principles of work study', or the procedure that the armed services use for 'appreciation of the situation' and giving orders. This is not surprising, since all sound working depends on the same underlying logic, which in fact goes back to Aristotle.[2] For working with clients in a task-centred way, a specialised procedure like this is ideal. Some of its stages (like planning, action and review) are universal, but others, like 'establishing mandate for work' apply specifically to the worker–client interaction. But social workers — and still more, managers — have a wide variety of tasks to carry out — supervision, motivation, report-writing, negotiation etc. What they need is a series of steps that apply in getting *any* job done.

'Tackle a task'

The basic steps of carrying out *any* task are:[3]

1. *Aims* — why the job is being done, and what specific result is wanted.

2. *Information* about
   - Means and resources for doing the job
   - Obstacles
   - Consequences and risk. What can be lost if the job goes wrong? What are the risks of inaction or delay?
   (For each of these headings, (i) assemble information available (facts or ideas), and (ii) find out whatever else is needed.)

3. *Planning.* Deciding *what* is to be done, and *who* is to do it, how, when and where.

4. *Action* — doing it!

5. *Review.* Checking (a) whether the job is complete, and to standard; and (b) what has been learnt for other occasions.

This sequence is called 'Tackle a Task' (TaT). It is not only a guide for action, but a description of how people are forced to work in practice, since if they tackle a job out of sequence, they will be dragged back to the stage they have missed out. If you start on a task before the aims are clear, you may be heading totally in the wrong direction. If you make plans before you have the information, you may find out too late that your assumptions are wrong, and your plans have hole in them. If you blunder into action without at least rudimentary planning, you may have to scrap what you have done and start again. In a task where the risk is high, the results can be disastrous — for yourself or your client. Problems like this are not unknown in social work. For example:

- Arrangements being made for a mother and child to enter a family centre — without clarifying why this is necessary
- Failing to gather information on a child's extended family (as the Children Act requires) before applying for a court order.

The sequence applies at all levels — not merely in individual social work, but in supervision and management. Take first the simplest example: a key worker, discussing a problem with two volunteers. The problem concerns Grant, a young white man with learning difficulties, living in supported accommodation. He is not very good at getting about on his own, and the *task* the co-ordinator sets the volunteers is: to teach Grant to go by bus to the leisure centre on his own.

Together they pose the question of *aims*. Why do we want Grant to take himself to the leisure centre? Various aims are suggested:

- to reduce Grant's dependence on other people
- to improve his social performance
- to enable him to function in the community.

These aims are all related, and the task can go some way towards achieving all of them. (As is normal, aims lie beyond the task, which is only one step towards them.)

The group then look at the *information*: what is Grant capable of doing already, and what specific problems does he have (handling money, dealing with people)? What means are available for overcoming the problems? The obvious approach is to encourage Grant to build up skills and confidence step by step, rewarding him with praise when he is successful. What is the risk, if it goes wrong? In this case the risk is fairly low; as long as Grant isn't put off buses for life, if the first attempt fails, he can always try again.

Having the information, you draw up a *plan*. Of the two volunteers, Hilda will go on Saturday, and Joe on Tuesday. Joe will supervise the first trial. He will agree plans with Grant in advance, making sure he has the exact money: arrange to get on the bus behind him and sit close by, but not talk unless Grant runs into trouble. After the journey, he will check with Grant how he felt. He will report the results to Hilda by phone, and if all goes well she will repeat the process on Saturday.

The next stage is *Action*: on Tuesday and Saturday, Joe and Hilda carry out the plan.

The *review*, involving both volunteers and the key worker, follows in a week's time. Did the trials succeed? What was the effect on Grant? Were there any problems, or unexpected successes? The Review will produce information, from which the next phase in Grant's development can be planned.

TaT in briefing

One serious problem for managers and supervisers is to balance the demands of a task against the skill and experience of the worker or volunteer who will carry it out. It is easy to overestimate people's expertise, especially with students or volunteers. It is crucial for their confidence to give them enough guidance to get the job right first time; on the other hand if you fuss round and overdo the help, morale may suffer even more. If they are dealing with clients, there is always the chance that they will set off consequences they hadn't expected and may not know how to handle. One major benefit of TaT is that it can be used by managers as a guideline for briefing.

The rule is, the less the experience of the person being briefed, the further through TaT you need to go. If someone is already expert, they can simply be told the task, and left to get on with it. To an experienced volunteer the key worker might say 'Why not get Grant gradually used to travelling alone by bus'. With someone less experienced, the key worker may need to check through the aims, and perhaps provide some of the information. 'The idea is to gradually build up the things Grant can do. Getting himself some-where by bus is a good starting point: you could arrange to be nearby in support, but get him to pay his own fare.' With a beginner, the manager will need to go through aims, information and plan in detail, and perhaps supervise the action.

The format can often be useful when giving out a job that is complex or delicate, or one that may be unpopular. Suppose a manager has to introduce ethnic record-keeping, the reaction of her team may be fairly hostile, a tendency to query the aims and identify obstacles: it isn't needed, it will take too long, and certainly won't help us. The manager's response should be to go through the process patiently, inviting the team to give their own answers to each stage, but providing answers if the team can't or won't. The resulting chart might read:

Task. Keep records of clients' ethnic origins.

Aims. To help us evaluate needs and deliver appropriate services: e.g. interpreting; providing literature in the right languages; know-ing how many places are needed in residential homes that provide a Muslim diet.

Information
Means. System of records provided by head office.

Obstacles	*Overcome by*
System takes too long	Measuring time actually taken, and setting time aside
Involves asking embarrassing questions	Explaining purpose to clients
Categories aren't right (where do we put Tibetans?)	Making representations to head office and getting guidance
No benefits to us at local level.	Defining what analysis could be useful locally, and approaching steering group.

Plan	*Who?*	*By when?*
1. Approach steering group, about (i) ethnic categories included, and (ii) analysis needed locally.	Manager	Tuesday
2. Try out the form, get consumer reactions and estimate of how long it takes	Aaron and Melanie	2 weeks
3. Forms to be distributed to all staff: notice in reception area as a reminder.	Admin Asst.	Today
4. Check forms against visitors' record, and remind delinquent staff!	Admin Asst.	Daily

Review in 4 weeks' time.

Stages in detail; distinction and overlap

(a) it is sometimes useful to use the stages of doing a task as a deliberate procedure: 'We have all the information, so now let's make a plan'. It is always useful to be aware of what stage you are at — and where other people are. Some people are impatient with planning, and are always rushing into action: others are more cautious or sluggish, and reluctant to move. A common understanding of the work sequence can help them sort out their differences and can arbitrate between them. Is the information all there, and the plan complete? If so, it's time for action, and there's no argument.

(b) The information stage is complex.

- Under the main headings (Means, Obstacles, Consequences (including Risk), you need to assemble the information you have, and find out whatever is missing. The progress of the task may be held up at this point — you may need to go out and get information, before you can plan.
- 'Information' can include not only facts, but also ideas and possibilities — which may need to be tested before live action.
- A further sort of information that is often useful is Cause and Effect. If for example a parent has bouts of alcoholism, it is important to know what triggers the behaviour off. It may be equally useful to know some of the effects of the behaviour — e.g. that a child in the family responds to it by causing trouble at school. Sometimes cause and effect are connected by a feedback loop, so that the causality is circular. Within a

family, the behaviour of one member may be caused by the outbursts of another — which they themselves have triggered off. This is an important concept in family therapy.[4]

- Sometimes the information stage will contain a complex process of weighing up pros and cons. Intervening in a family is an uncertain business, and may have complex effects, both good and bad; these effects may be probable, or only remote possibilities. It is safe to say that the higher the risk, the longer the information stage needs to take, perhaps including dry runs or simulated action (for the crucial question of risk, see section on p. 26).

(c) Where a task is vague or complex, there may be some overlap between the aims and information stages, since information may be needed before the aims can be established. If a manager is simply told to 'Get over there and sort things out', she will have to find out what's wrong before she knows what she's trying to achieve. Again it may be difficult to set detailed targets or success criteria until the planning stage, since you may have to know how you intend to act before you can pin down what constitutes success.

(d) The difference between Information and Planning is not always obvious, but there is a simple test: a plan is what one has definitely decided to do — a series of instructions to oneself or the team. As long as a course of action is only a possibility, it remains 'information'. (The distinction can be important when several people have to co-operate, but each is pushing their own ideas.)

Tackle a Task in cycles

Sometimes one can follow the sequence through and finish a task in one bite. More often people work through a series of cycles — they get some of the information, make a rudimentary plan, carry it out, and then realise, in review, that the job is only half done. They then get more information and have another go (the aim remaining constant throughout). This is the natural, human way of working, and it is often effective: we feel our way gradually, taking one step at a time (this is the approach being adopted towards Grant.) It can be shown by a diagram (Fig. 2.2).

To give an example. A borough contracts out some of its mental health care to an independent day centre. You believe the centre is doing its best according to its lights, but the clients seem apathetic or bored. You set yourself the task, 'increase range of activities offered to users'. A note of progress over the next few weeks might read:

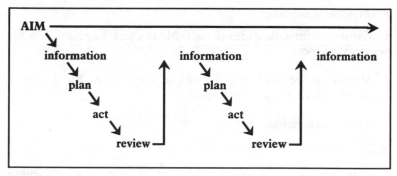

Figure 2.2

Aims — why?

- To increase the stimulus to users, giving
  (a) better therapy and
  (b) more fun.
- To give users a chance to develop skills that could be used outside the centre, in developing hobbies and/or social life: possibly to use at work.

Information
Obstacles:

- Users seem to spend 90 per cent of their time making Christmas cards.
- Manager is touchy, and proud of his work — though genuinely committed.

Means:

- Sell the idea to manager; explain the aims and let him draw his own conclusions.
- In the last resort we *could* take our clients away, but the last thing we want is to set up our own centre.

Plan
Approach manager with tactful enthusiasm. Meeting fixed for 9.6.93.

Action

Review → Information

- At the meeting, the manager accepted the aims, and we discussed possibilities. Learning point: explaining the aims worked well.

Plans made at meeting:

1. Manager to introduce idea to staff. Me to check by phone how his presentation went.

2. Meeting to be held to get views of users (fixed for 21.6.93). Manager will chair it and I will speak.

Action — two meetings held.

Reviews

1. Manager reports reluctance of staff to co-operate. Learning points: don't neglect staff of contracting organisations: managers may not be much good at selling ideas they only half accept.

2. Users seemed to be very pleased. General agreement that they would like to do something with music.

Information needed: Who can run a good music class? etc.

Risk and contrasting approaches

Many projects, including most long-term ones, involve feeling your way through cycles of action, review and replanning. There are however some pieces of work where you can't operate like this: those where the first action commits you, so you have only one chance. (An example of a one-chance task is baking a soufflé — if you over-cook it, you can't undo it. Compare making salad dressing, where if there's too much oil, you can always add vinegar.) What makes the difference is *risk*, in the special sense of 'what do you lose if action is wrong and you have to start again?' In this sense, making a soufflé, though trivial in itself, is high-risk — if you cook it too long, you lose the lot. The difference between these two kinds of task is fundamental, since it determines the approach: in a job where you have many chances, you can work by trial and error; a one-chance task has to be approached with caution and complete preparation. Compare the case in social work. Here most tasks are far from trivial, and risks, in the sense of potential damage to clients, are very high. But even here there are many tasks that are low-risk, in the sense that you can work by trial and error. In working over a period with a family with multiple difficulties, trial and review is not only the best approach, but the only one. You are aiming here at gradual improvement, and the individual steps are often low-risk: you can, for example, go back again to get more details on the extent of their debts. On the other hand, if you are considering applying for an emergency protection order, the risk is very high — get it wrong, and it may be irrevocable.

Yet another aspect of risk is unpredictability. By and large if you are dealing with mechanical things, like causes bring like results — run out of petrol and the car stops. The reactions of human beings are far less predictable — especially those of people who are somewhat unstable, or young — which is why, in dealing with clients, the possible consequences have to be evaluated with particular care.

In a high-risk task, there are certain things you can do to make the risk less:

- Check and recheck information and plans;
- Identify the step that constitutes the point of no-return, and review before you take it;
- Where possible, carry out a rehearsal or dummy run. This not only checks the soundness of your plans, but also allows practice, so developing skill and confidence.

Summary: some benefits of using Tackle a Task

- For self-organising: it leads you in a natural sequence towards action, and tells you when to take the plunge.
- For co-ordinating: it keeps people's thinking in step.
- For diagnosis: it helps you see why a meeting has got out of step (e.g. trying to plan before the aims are agreed).
- For delegating — a checklist of how much help to give.
- As a guide in uncharted territory — you don't know yet how to tackle a problem, but you can work your way systematically towards action. This applies particularly in the most uncharted area of all — planning to improve relations with other people.
- As a pattern for learning from experience, by reviewing and re-planning to do better.

2.2 Aims

Types of aims

Of the five stages of Tackle a Task, the most complex and important is 'Aims'. If aims are clear and agreed, action will usually follow: but if aims are unclear, or in conflict, not much can usefully be done.

Aims are of two main sorts:

1. The *purpose* for which the job is being done. We are re-housing Mrs Jones, *in order to prevent her having to climb stairs.*

The way to discover purpose is by asking why? Why re-house Mrs Jones? In order to prevent her climbing stairs. Note that a purpose can always be preceded by the phrase 'in order to'. If the answer given was *'because* she has a heart condition' it would provide not an aim — which reaches into the future, but a statement of cause, reaching back into the past.

2. The result or *target* that is aimed at — which may be described as the 'objective', 'end product', 'assignment' or 'remit'. Some kinds of tasks have a definite ending point — for example, 'introduce a new record-keeping system', or 'help Mrs Jones' daughter find a job'. Other tasks never end: for example, the task of running a children's home. For these, continuous tasks, the target takes the form of a level of quality or **'standard'**: the result being looked for is that children are, and go on being, well-fed, happy and tolerably well behaved. Standards need not only relate to results — they can also relate to the way in which the task is done (**'performance standards'**). In running a children's home, a performance standard, not directly related to results, might be that at least two members of staff are qualified.

The point of being clear on aims is to let people know precisely where they are trying to get to, and how they can tell whether they have succeeded. The target alone may not make this clear: the target may be something like 'higher morale within the department', but how will you know that morale is higher? You may therefore need a third kind of aim — a pre-set *indicator of success*. This is a way of telling whether the outcome has been achieved. If the outcome being sought is higher morale, one indicator might be a reduction in sick leave, or in use of the grievance procedure. Indicators, like standards, can apply either to results or to the way the job is done (**'performance indicators'**).

Since terms for aims are often inconsistent — one person's 'aim' being another's 'objective' and vice versa, it is often safer to use a phrase 'What exactly are we trying to achieve, and why do we want it? In this book, terms are used as follows:

Aims — a generic term covering all the following.
1. Purpose: the aim for the sake of which the task is being done; usually something outside and beyond the task.
2. Target. A statement of what is being asked for, including:
— in a task that can be completed, the result wanted or **end product**.
— in a continuous task, the **standard** that is looked for. This may relate to:
— The way the job is done (e.g. 'using qualified staff').
— The level of performance (e.g. 'meals are always hot').
— The results of the job (e.g. user satisfaction).

3. Indicators of success.   Precise (preferably quantifiable) signs by which the success of the task can be judged, including:
— **result indicators**
— **performance indicators**
— **progress indicators.**   In a long completable task, a way of seeing that you are on track — e.g. half way by half-time.
Finally most indicators have to be quantified, and turned into:
4. Measures.   The monitoring/inspection process can take the form of **sample tests**, to find out whether the measures are being achieved.

Open and closed aims

Aims can be 'open' — in the sense of being vague or ill-defined — or closed, in the sense of being narrow and definite. A client can come into a social services department with a closed aim to 'get twenty pounds out of them' or a much more open one — 'give my kid a better chance'. A lot of the art of management (or self-management) consists of converting open aims into closed ones — turning a vague sense of unease into a specific intention. It often happens that a social worker will come and talk over a case with her superviser, without being at all clear on what the aims of the intervention ought to be. The same problem can crop up with referrals from other agencies — it may be hard for referrers to put their finger on what needs doing. In one case the concern expressed by both the school and the health visitor came down to the fact that a mother never collected her children from school. The first question for the social worker was what were the aims of any step she took? Was it to improve the children's safety on the way home, or to reduce the responsibility (for running the household etc.) being put on their shoulders? Or was it perhaps to help the mother, because of a suspicion that she was becoming withdrawn and unable to cope. It would be hard to get the intervention right without being clear what it was meant to achieve.
Aims can be 'open' in three different ways:

1. When the purpose is unclear. Ask *why* are we doing it?
2. When the result wanted is unclear. Ask *what* exactly would make a satisfactory result.
3. The *amount* wanted is unclear. If the task of a volunteer is to visit an elderly woman, make it clear how many visits a week are expected.

Aims and conflict

When people who need to co-operate find that their aims are in conflict, not much can be done until the conflict is resolved. Conflicts are often latent, as sometimes in case-work, where several different agencies are involved, each with different aims laid down by statute. Perhaps the most obvious example, on which a lot of work has been done, is in cases of child abuse, where social workers have a duty to protect the child, while the police have a duty to get a conviction. Here the conflict of aims is obvious, though particularly difficult to resolve, but there may be more subtle differences of priority. Take the example of a boy with learning difficulties, who has suffered neglect at home. The social worker may be concerned to rehabilitate him within his own family, while a teacher may be pressing to keep him at boarding school, for the sake of his education. Again health visitors may be concerned with questions of long-term health that can seem irrelevant to a social worker who is trying to deal with immediate family stress. Even within a social services department, people from different sections — such as home helps — may see problems in a very different light.

The cure with most conflicts of aims is to get them in the open, and look for a course of action that will suit both sides. Is it somehow possible to provide special schooling without breaking up the family? It is a good thing if potential points of conflict can be discussed between agencies before actual clashes occur. The worst outcome is where different services pursue their own private agendas without communicating, until some radical disagreement suddenly comes to light at a case conference, with the client actually sitting there.

Levels of aims — the why/how network

This section describes a formal approach for handling work where aims are complex, obscure, or potentially in conflict.

Aims tend to arrange themselves in hierarchies: we do X in order to do Y in order to do Z. For example:

Re-house Mrs Jones.   Why?
In order to prevent her having to climb stairs.   Why?
In order to reduce the risk of a heart attack.

Sometimes aims branch. We might also wish to re-house Mrs Jones in order to locate her nearer to her daughter, and to give her a more practical journey to the shops.

The opposite of an aims statement is a statement of means, which is brought out by the question 'How?'

How do we reduce the risk of Mrs Jones having a heart attack?
By preventing her having to climb stairs.

How do we prevent her having to climb stairs?
By re-housing her.

The series of questions 'How' can be continued downwards.
How do we re-house Mrs Jones?

1. By contacting the Housing Department
2. By checking with the XYZ Housing Association.

A group of aims like these can be arranged to form a network[5]
(Fig. 2.3).

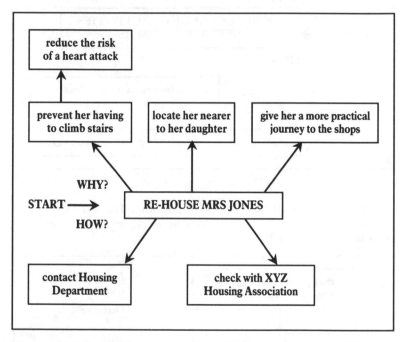

(By convention, 'Whys' go upwards, and 'Hows' go downwards).

Figure 2.3

In the case of the day centre on page 24, the aims of the social worker
can be presented by the same sort of network (Fig. 2.4).

As an aims network shows, the distinction between aims, objectives
and tasks depends on where you stand. The Task is the job you are set
to do. The Purpose is something beyond the task — the box one or two
levels higher up in the network. Often my purpose is my boss's 'task': I
am doing my part of the job to contribute towards the wider aims for

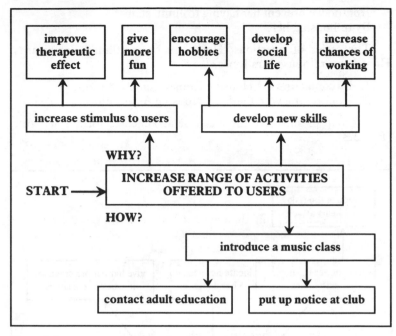

Figure 2.4

which more senior management is responsible. The 'ethnic records'
task on page 22 can be shown as a network, with the staff level
responsible beside each box:

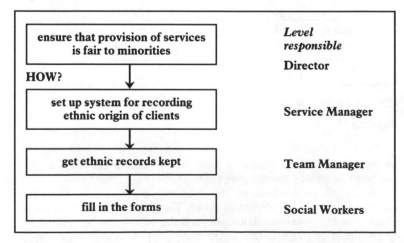

Figure 2.5

The *task* of social workers is to fill in the form, but their *aim* is to ensure fairness — the task of the director.

A network has the following uses:

- For clarifying aims and means when starting a complex project.
- For opening the mind to a range of possibilities. It is for example a useful basis for brain-storming when a range of different solutions may be needed — 'how else can we get favourable publicity?'
- To encourage a democratic approach to aim-setting and planning, allowing everyone to take part (for an example see page 79).
- As a basis for setting success or performance measures.
- For reconciling aims. Sometimes people may be in short-term conflict, but their higher-level aims may be identical (police and social workers both want to reduce child-abuse). Occasionally you find the opposite — people's long-term aims are diametrically opposed, but they can agree on a short-term step that will suit them both — such as going to arbitration.

2.3   Targets, end products and success measures

A target is a specific statement of what a task is intended to achieve. It may be:

1. the end-product, or
2. a way-mark: a stage towards achieving the result, or
3. a sample test of something that is bound to happen before success is achieved.

Taking the case studies in the first part of this chapter, some targets the social worker might set are as follows:

For Grant

- Within two weeks: being able to buy his ticket on the bus to the leisure centre, provided he has the right money, and a volunteer is present.
- Within four weeks: being able to travel to the leisure centre alone.

    These are both interim targets. There could also be a longer-term one — e.g. that within six months, Grant should be able to travel anywhere by local bus. How useful this will be for the volunteers depends on the scope they are allowed:

there may be little point in setting a long-term target if they are being checked up on every five minutes. It is however important for the social worker to set *herself* long-term targets, to highlight whether intended improvements are in fact happening.

For ethnic record-keeping

* Over the next month, the ethnic background of 90 per cent of clients will be recorded (compared with at present 25 per cent).

For the Day Centre

* Within 3 months at least one new activity (music) will have been introduced.
* Within 6 months there should be at least six different activities, from which users can select three.
* At least three activities can be carried on at home, and at least two actively encourage socialising.

The last kind of target — a sample test — is most useful for the sort of indefinite task that is most difficult to quantify. Some of the aims of the day centre project are that users should have more fun, and be able and willing to try out day centre activities in their own time. How do you measure fun? There is no point in introducing music or whatever if it is run in such a way that everyone hates it. Some kind of rudimentary sample or survey is needed, on the lines of: at the end of 6 months I will select six random long-term users, and ask them whether they are enjoying themselves more: the target being, at least three yeses, and not more than one no. Or it might be more objective to set targets relating to attendance levels.

The benefits of setting targets

1. People know precisely what is wanted, and what to aim for. If interim targets are set, they know they are on track to get there.
2. People know when a job is finished, and no more needs to be done.
3. Targets have a powerful effect on morale. People who know that they are on track — or what they must do to get back on track — are likely to work confidently and effectively. By contrast, people without clear targets may not know if they are succeeding or failing. They are dependent on their boss for reassurance or guidance, and if the boss herself has no firm

criteria, they may feel that they are dependent on her caprice, rather than having objective goals.

If a target is to be useful in these ways, it must be objective, and as precise as possible, and this often means quantified. It is no use setting someone a target of 'reducing travelling costs *substantially*: the target must specify the amount and timing — 'a reduction of £3,000 over the next six months'.

Setting targets is just as valuable for managers, since they make it much easier to monitor results. If the right targets are identified — the things that make the difference between success and failure — the manager can simply ask for periodical reports, and be less dependent on the sort of close supervision that staff may resent as fussing.

From the point of view of morale, the best targets are those that are self-set. There is evidence that people who are allowed to set their own targets tend to set more stretching ones than their own managers would regard as reasonable. Moreover they are committed to reaching them, not wanting to let themselves down, and they have no one to blame except themselves if they fail.

One crucial use of targets is in quality control. Suppliers of services under contract are in some ways in a similar position to employees: they may be more or less committed to doing a good job, and having clear objectives will tend to motivate them. They may well, in certain cases, be guided into setting targets for themselves. The clearer and more comprehensive the targets that are set, the easier is the job of monitoring results (for quality assurance, see chapter 5).

2.4   Aims and policy in social work

Drawing up statements of policy is now a key step in the overall management of social services. It is also a good demonstration of how the TaT sequence underlies the process of management, even at the highest level. Here fundamental aims are set by the government, and amplified by local authorities: the information stage consists of assessing need and comparing it with existing services; the outcome is a plan, which will determine the actions of the social services department over the next twelve months. This section looks first at what a policy statement for a local authority is required to contain, then at how some of the elements can be useful, both in managing a local authority department and also for suppliers.

2.5 Policy and planning — the statutory basis

In community care, policy statements are now required by law (see *Caring for People* (1990) and the National Health Service and Community Care Act 1990, section 46). Social services departments have a duty to consult users and also the independent sector, and must plan in close collaboration with Health Authorities. These plans must be published on a yearly basis (the deadline for the first plan having been April 1992), and will be monitored by the Social Services Inspectorate. Child care plans began to be produced in the mid 1980s, and most authorities now have them,[6] sometimes integrated with their Community Care plans. Child protection procedures are agreed on an inter-disciplinary basis by Area Child Protection Committees.

2.6 Who sets policy?

National policy for social services is set by government and has statutory backing. From time to time the Government issues further statements, showing what it regards as the current priorities. Within these terms of reference, local authorities decide on local priorities, based on their assessment of local needs, and draw up an overall plan, so that work can be delegated to the appropriate departments and sections. However these mustn't be treated as immutable: since priorities change, the organisation of social services may need to change with them, and authorities must check that their organisation is still the right one to deliver the goods. What complicates the whole process is that funds are inevitably limited, and the local authority has to take account of this, both in setting priorities and in deciding on the level of service to be provided. The whole process can be shown by a diagram (Fig. 2.6).

(The division of responsibilities between councillors and officers is not as clear-cut as shown, since on most issues, officers recommend and councillors may or may not agree. However in the normal way (as shown in the diagram) politicians *should* decide on the aims, while being guided by officers on means.)

2.7 What goes into a policy statement

A policy statement may include:

- A statement of the organisation's mission and core values.

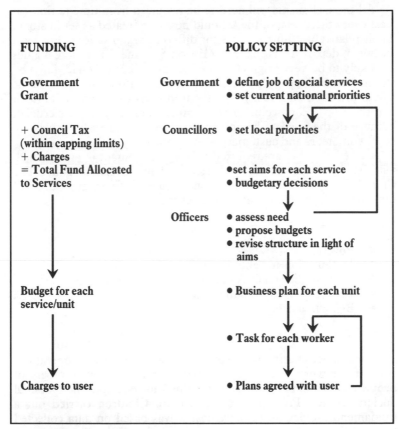

FUNDING   POLICY SETTING

Government   Government   • define job of social services
Grant   • set current national priorities

+ Council Tax   Councillors   • set local priorities
(within capping limits)
+ Charges
= Total Fund Allocated   •set aims for each service
to Services   • budgetary decisions

                    Officers   • assess need
                                • propose budgets
                                • revise structure in light of
                                  aims

Budget for each   • Business plan for each unit
service/unit

                                • Task for each worker

Charges to user   • Plans agreed with user

Figure 2.6

This should be succinct and memorable, and known to everyone who works in the service or uses it.

- Aims and objectives
  (a) For the service as a whole — e.g. political decisions on priorities; also policy on equal opportunities, covering both employment, and delivery of services.[7]
  (b) For each service or major sub-division.
- Strategic plans, including timescales
- Standards to be reached for quality assurance
- Day-to-day procedures; practice guidelines
- Systems for monitoring.

It will probably *not* include job descriptions, or detailed working plans, specifying who does what.

All these elements will need to be reviewed from time to time (at least every three years): they should never be treated as set in stone. Their relative usefulness varies for different organisations. For local authority departments, neither Mission Statement nor Core Values are likely to be very original, since they are effectively laid down by statute, backed up by professional training: they can however be useful provided staff really take them to heart (and can quote them in discussion). For a voluntary or commercial body, they are crucial, because of the need to be absolutely clear — and make it clear to staff, volunteers and customers — what the body is there to provide. Registered charities are required to have a statement of aims, which will usually be amplified by decisions of its governing body. The Children's Society, for example, concentrates on five main sources of injustice or deprivation that may affect children:

- Poverty
- Exploitation and abuse
- Being denied choice or control over their own lives
- Being removed from their own homes
- Being in custody.

For a major charity, reviewing its mission can be a big operation, since if the work is done in a democratic way, great numbers of people have to express their view. When for example the National Society for the Prevention of Cruelty to Children carried out a fundamental review of its activities, it was based on data collected through thousands of questionnaires, and nine regional conferences were held to discuss the issues. The effects too were far-reaching: it was decided that the Society's job was to concentrate on the core work of presenting child abuse of the severest kind. As a result it became clear that a number of its activities, such as 'Listen to Children' week, though valuable and successful in themselves, were only peripheral to its essential aims, and as a result they were discontinued.[8]

The Policy Statement needs to be readable and not too bulky. It is likely to have a core section followed by sections for each specific service. It may need to be produced in different formats (and languages) for different classes of reader, including short, clear booklets for users. All versions should use charts and diagrams to explain, and make a clear division between plans for different client groups, so that no one need plough through material that doesn't concern them.

Notes

1 Doel, M., Marsh, P. (1992) *Task-Centred Social Work* Ashgate.
2 For 'practical reasoning and its relation to scientific method and modern formulae for getting work done', see Taylor (1990b).
3 For TaT, see Taylor (1990b). TaT is based on 'A Systematic Approach to Getting Things Done', long used in Coverdale Training (Taylor, 1992).
4 See Ross, S., Bilson, A. (1989) *Social Work Management and Practice.*
5 The Why/How network was first derived by G.E.M. Anscombe from Aristotle's Practical Reasoning (Anscombe 1954). Its practical use was developed by The Coverdale Organisation (Taylor 1992).
6 The Department of Health publication *Child Care Policy: putting it in writing* (1990) shows that 73 out of 92 Social Service Departments returned examples of child care policies.
7 In the REU survey on equal opportunities policies, 92 out of 133 authorities responded. Of these, 57 had a policy for service delivery, while 44 included policies for race equality *Equally Fair* (see Butt *et al.*, 1991).
8 For The Children's Society and The National Society for the Prevention of Cruelty to Children, see Taylor 1992.

3 Assessment of need and marketing

3.1 Marketing, in business and in social work

'The purpose of a business', says a management classic[1], 'is to provide something for which an independent outsider, who can choose not to buy, is willing to exchange his purchasing power.' 'Marketing' means making this process possible: determining what the organisation can provide, and who is likely to buy it, at what price; identifying opportunities, potential competition, and how we can make our product be seen as uniquely valuable. It is a complex process, at the heart of commercial business.

The work of a social services department is different in almost every way. Its customers are not 'totally independent': they have little choice of where to look for help, and in seeking help, no purchasing power. The department has no need to attract customers, and no competitors to fight off. To talk of 'marketing' is therefore something of a misnomer. The one aspect of marketing that is not only relevant but crucial is the job of discovering what customers really want, and finding ways of satisfying them.

The position of the actual providers of services — whether voluntary or commercial — is far different: indeed they are in much the same position as ordinary businesses. They have two special marketing problems which are unusual, though not unique: first, they may have only one customer — their local social services department; secondly, the person who buys their services — the social worker — is not actually the user. This means that, in a commercial sense, it is more important to satisfy the social services department than the people the service is intended to benefit. Which brings us back to the conclusion of the last paragraph — the need to find out what customers really want, and whether they are getting it.

3.2 Defining need

The NHS and Community Care Act states that 'Social Services Departments will be expected to set out the needs of the population they serve'; similarly the Children Act places a duty on local authorities to identify 'children in need'. The Acts therefore aim to introduce a rational approach to planning, such as has not been evident since the period immediately after the Seebohm report. This represents a shift in the responsibilities of Social Services Departments, which Juliet Cheetham has described as 'an unmissable chance to proclaim common human needs, which could — and should — be addressed by social policy'.[2]

The problem is, however, that neither of the Acts provide much guidance on what 'need' actually means: it is left to the local authorities and the profession to set up its own dialogue. The issue is partly a philosophical one — out of the enormous variety of human unhappiness, which should we try to alleviate? — and partly political — what is being asked for, and what is public opinion prepared to provide? The section below can't provide the answers, but it can pose some of the questions.

What kinds of need are there?

One kind of classification is essentially *political*, based on who is demanding what.[3] One can distinguish between:

1. **Felt need** — needs that people are aware of, whether or not they ask for help. (Women looking after disabled relatives have needed support for centuries, without pushing their need into public consciousness.)
2. **Expressed need** — what people ask for. An expressed need may be taken up by public opinion or pressure groups, and converted into:
3. **Organised demand** — active political pressure. Eventually demands may gather into a tide of frustration that will persuade public authorities that the need must be met. As a result of many years in which elderly residents have demanded single rooms, this is now accepted as a valid need in residential care. The result of acceptance is:

4. **Normative need** — that defined by official policy statements. An elderly person may be defined as 'in need' of a
telephone if she meets the department's criteria of being both
housebound and isolated.
5. **Comparative need** — What people see being provided
elsewhere. The need may be demonstrated statistically: the
Social Services Committee may be presented with figures to show
that there is a 'need' for more home placements with black
families, because there are more black children in long-term
residential care than there are in the next door authority, which
has a similar population profile.

These distinctions throw no light on how needs can be compared
or ranked. The alternative is a philosophical categorisation, as
proposed by Doyal and Gough[4] in an attempt to arrive at a universal
theory of human need. They propose a universal goal of *avoidance of
serious harm* combined with *the capacity for social participation*. For
these to be achieved, there are two further basic needs:

Survival and physical health — defined as the absence of disease,
and
Autonomy — defined as the ability to make informed choices
about what should be done and how to go about doing it. They
then list a number of intermediate needs, which will be satisfied
in different ways and to different levels in different societies.

For the social services context, we suggest the following categories of intermediate needs.

1. **Physiological needs** — things the body must have to stay
alive and healthy: water, food, warmth. Closely related to this are
medical needs — the absence or relief of injury, disease and
pain.
2. **Physical needs**: material things needed for daily living
(housing, transport etc.) — adapted to take account of any
physical disabilities.
3. **Psychological needs**: things needed for mental balance and
competence, and the chance of happiness.
4. **Social needs**: including (a) individual social needs — things
people must have to take a full part in society (education, forms
of freedom and autonomy, rights of citizenship, absence of
unjust discrimination), and (b) collective social needs — law,
public security, government and public services.

The next stage is to decide which sorts of need (out of the variety
of sufferings) fall to the social services to put right. Any such
demarcation must consider the following elements.

1. Quality and extent of the need

Needs dealing with such categories as:

- Threats to life, or to physical or mental health
- Pain or long-term physical discomfort
- Denial of a satisfactory upbringing (in terms of love, stimulus, education, stability and freedom from cruelty and other abuse)
- Physical or mental inability to do things that society regards as a necessary part of decent living
- Deprivation of possessions/experiences that society regards as a necessary part of decent living
- Deep unhappiness or severe mental discomfort.

2. Urgency or risk

- Things happening now
- Things that will certainly happen, unless action is taken
- Things that may happen unless action is taken — qualified by probability, likelihood of delay, and early warning signs.

3. Ways of alleviating the need

The need must:

- Not be readily alleviated by the sufferer's own efforts, taking account of their age, physical and mental state, and personal resources.
- Not be the responsibility of some other service or public resource, or the enforceable responsibility of some private body or individual. (For example, responsibilities of the health, housing or employment services; matters that should be dealt with by employers, landlords, insurance or the courts — though delay in response could bring the case back to the social services.)
- Be able to be alleviated at proportionate cost.
- Be able to be met by means that are socially acceptable.

Some social services committees, and some members of the public, might add a fourth category — the degree to which the client deserves help. This has a long history, going back to the allocation of charitable funds in the nineteenth century. In current thinking, neither the Acts nor local policy follow this distinction, but it is still evident in the deliberations of private charities and frequently implicit in social work decisions.

Official definitions of need must take account of resources available, but they shouldn't be totally constricted by them. In several authorities, wide definitions of 'need' under the Children Act have been considered during the consultation process, but something much narrower has been accepted as being 'realistic' in the light of resources. This brings us back to the framework, originally outlined by Curnock and Hardiker,[5] of social work assessment as a balance sheet of risk, needs and resources. Risk is often the predominant consideration; if risk is high, resources will be made available, but in situations of low risk, the worker should still make a careful assessment of need, before considering the available resources. A needs-led assessment cannot discount the importance of resources or deny the relevance of risk but it can seek to shift the balance between them.

The way policy can change meaning has been demonstrated in the controversy about recording unmet need in community care assessments. The Department of Health warned social services that if they failed to meet needs identified by the assessment, they could be legally liable under the Disabled Persons Act, and suggested that needs should not be recorded on individual clients' forms at all, but merely aggregated in total. This seemed to be flatly contrary to the intention of the Act. A later circular suggested that assessments should record clients' 'choices' rather than needs — so limiting the term 'need' to what the authority is prepared to provide.

These arguments underlie the process of setting priority categories of need. One authority[6] for example defines Priority Category 1, requiring a response within twenty-four hours, as *a threat to survival*; 'Client at acute or immediate risk to life or of rapid deterioration' or 'strong probability of deterioration and risk without intervention', and gives such examples as breakdown in care arrangements, acute physical deterioration, acute mental health episode, or actual or potential abuse. Category 2 then focusses on *improved quality of life*, and service planning to prevent future deterioration (relating to the basic needs for autonomy, provision of choice and opportunities for social participation). Some examples are a planned change of placement, or supporting a carer who is under stress.

For the social work manager, these arguments are not just academic. Departmental policy (or the business plan of a voluntary body) sets out normative definitions of need. There will always be a gap between these and the felt and expressed needs of individuals and community groups, and the social workers have to cope with the shortfall in expectations, while feeding evidence of unmet need back into the planning process.

Gathering information on need

A great deal of information about need can be discovered by aggregating the records of individual assessments. For this to be possible, assessment must follow a standard procedure, and records must be kept of what people say they need, not merely of services provided. Care managers will only keep to the procedure if they see that their returns have a real influence on planning. The whole process of assessment and response can be shown by a diagram (Fig. 3.1).

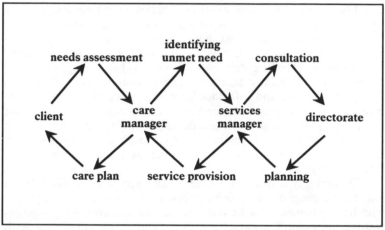

Figure 3.1

At each level there is a cyclical process of assessment, planning and review in which staff and users can be involved. To give an example, a succession of individual child care plans may suggest that there is a shortage of foster families for black children of various ethnic and cultural groups. The plans are collated by the service manager and compared with existing resources, to identify the gaps. The service manager consults voluntary organisations, and a range of groups in the black communities, and suggests what should be done: either more foster placements should be found, or independent providers should be encouraged to supply more places in small children's homes run by black staff. These options will be considered by the Directorate, in the light of the Children Act and the department's policy, and costs will be compared with other priorities. Once the decision has been taken, it will be published and explained to community groups, and form part of the guidelines which social workers follow in drawing-up individual care plans.

Community Care plans try to map out existing needs and resources, and to get a picture of future demands. From this one can estimate how demand may change, and suggest different ways in which services might develop, and at what cost. The broad decisions on priorities are essentially political, but it is up to local service managers to decide on individual cases in the light of these.

Community profiles

The purpose of a community profile is to identify pockets of unmet need, and so to re-plan the pattern of service delivery. In an ideal situation, both health and social care needs would be defined by a comprehensive local audit. One such was carried out in Leeds,[7] using Doyal and Gough's taxonomy of need to develop a questionnaire which was used widely with professionals, community groups and residents. The alternative to this comprehensive approach is a set of local community profiles.[8] These combine hard data from statistical sources, and soft data from the views of clients and the impressions of professionals. Preparing one is a useful starting point for decentralised social work teams, which are trying to introduce a community approach. It can be just as valuable for authorities which have adopted a specialist structure, in planning services for particular client groups.

The first step is to decide on the community to be profiled. It can either be a geographical neighbourhood, or a community of people who have a common background or shared concerns. Geographical communities don't always have neat boundaries coinciding with administrative districts. People define communities subjectively, by what counts as 'local', or by some sense of belonging. Neither of these are static; daily habits can be altered by shops closing or the cancellation of a bus service. The word 'community' has nostalgic overtones, but in many urban areas a sense of community may be more evident to the eye of the professional beholder than in the experience of local people. Communities of interest may be based on a particular need — such as being HIV positive, or parents of children with a particular disability — or they may be based on religious, racial or cultural identity, or experience of poverty or discrimination. Once again communities of interest are unlikely to fit neatly into official categories.

Having identified the community, the next step is to gather whatever information is available from official sources. The census may be a starting point, and broad projections of population changes will be found in the Community Care plan. Unfortunately the neighbourhood you wish to profile is unlikely to coincide with a ward or enumeration district, but the census figures should give a broad indication of the breakdown of the population by age, sex and ethnic origin, making it possible to identify children under five, or old people over seventy living alone, and to estimate trends. Another way of using the census is to map levels of need according to various social indicators. There is normally a correlation between factors such as unemployment, overcrowding, infant mortality, family size, and the number of children in care, and this will give an indication of where services should be concentrated. Census data can be supplemented by other statistical information, such as education and health records. It is also important to make good use of the information contained in the department's own records. Referral sheets contain a mass of data, which until recently was rarely collated. The introduction of standardised assessment forms and the use of information technology will revolutionise the data available both to planners and individual workers.

You can now decide whether to examine particular unmet needs by conducting a local survey. Time may be a problem, but you may be able to get help from a local college by defining a piece of work which could be tackled by a group of students, or to go into partnership with a voluntary organisation or community group. In either case, the purpose and targets of the survey should be defined and agreed at the start.

Various methods of gathering information can be used:

- A short questionnaire can be distributed — for example, to parents of children with special needs at selected schools. The advantage is that the questionnaire can be widely distributed by head teachers or through the post; the disadvantage is that it is difficult to explain the point of the research, so that only a small proportion will be returned.
- People can be interviewed, using a questionnaire which allows space for expanded answers and additional comments. This method could be used to look at the needs of residents on a particular estate, or the take-up of services in a particular area. Face-to-face contact provides more information than a written questionnaire, but it takes time, and interviewers need to be carefully briefed.
- A small number of people can be interviewed in depth, using an open-ended interview with a set of prompts, and recording answers either by audio-tape or full written notes. This is a good way of finding out how satisfied users are with a particular service such as a women's resource centre, or of building up a picture of the needs and lifestyle of an unrecognised group, such as young women with disabilities. The difficulties are that the data are hard to collate, and the

people interviewed may not be representative.

- With groups who are hard to reach, such as drug users or homeless young people, a more informal style is needed. Personal contacts can be used to suggest further respondents.

- With users of a day centre or people in residential care, group discussions can be organised, to supplement information from individual interviews.

Whichever method is used, it is important not to raise false hopes of improvements in services. It is also important to feed the information back to respondents, to prevent them from feeling ignored.

The common pitfall with survey work is putting a great deal of effort into gathering information that is never used. It is important to be clear about timescales and objectives: even if you are collaborating with a college or voluntary group, as the initiator you need to define what results you expect, and by when. The college may have ancillary objectives, but the different agendas must be clearly defined and a realistic timescale worked out for each of them.

Hidden communities

Some ethnic minority communities have remained invisible to social services planners, in spite of a substantial presence in a particular area: the assumption has been that because few referrals were received, there was no demand for services. One example was a Bangladeshi community who were living in large numbers in an inner-city housing estate, but were totally unrepresented in referrals made to the local area team. When they noticed this, the team looked at the existing referral network and found that apart from a small number of white clients who referred themselves, the great majority were sent by other professionals. They decided to learn more about local community groups, and found that several of them had contacts with the Bangladeshi community. With the help of members of these groups who spoke Bengali, and understood Sylheti, and of some social work students, they carried out a small survey to find out what the Bangladeshi residents knew about social services, and followed this up with an open day to offer information and advice. As a result, the reception area was re-designed, and leaflets and posters were provided in community languages. The team applied for funding for a Bengali-speaking worker, and within the department, equality targets were reviewed to make the provision of services more suitable. At the request of the Bangladeshi women, the adult education service arranged English classes for them, with a woman teacher at a local centre, and helped the local Mosque to set up Bengali and Arabic classes for the children.

In this case the area team managed to reallocate the department's own resources. Sometimes the local authority may prefer to develop services in partnership with the voluntary sector. Research carried out by the National Institute of Social Work[9] on community care schemes found that partnership with a community group could give local people a greate᷈ sense of ownership and involvement. Another advantage of partnership schemes was that the local authority needs to only be involved at the start, since responsibility could then be handed over to a voluntary management committee. Sometimes the initiative will come from an existing voluntary organisation or community group. For example, a group of parents whose children went to a play group at a local community centre were concerned about the lack of out-of-school provision for children with special needs. With the help of a community centre worker, they circulated a questionnaire to other parents. They then set up a committee, which liaised with other voluntary groups and approached the education department and the social services disabilities team for help with setting up an after-school club. In another case a community settlement became concerned about the lack of help for women who were victims of domestic violence, and decided to look at the need for a telephone helpline. Because of the vulnerability of the victims, a survey wasn't practical, so need had to be assessed through contact with existing services, and through publicity and open meetings. An application for funding was then made to charitable trusts.

A carers' centre

A local authority may identify an unmet need and include it in its Community Care Plan, and then develop a service in partnership with a voluntary agency. It is a well-known danger of community care, that the whole burden of caring for elderly, disabled or confused people may fall on female relative᷈, who are caught between what society expects of them and their own sense of duty. They often get little support, either emotional or practical, and because their plight is hardly noticed, they could well be described as a hidden community. A local authority with a high population of elderly people, might decide to set up a support system for carers. As a start, a carer's group could be set up in a local day centre, and it could later develop into a drop-in centre and telephone helpline, staffed by a part-time worker and volunteers. The centre could have its own management committee, or it might start off as a project under the wing of the community centre; in either case help and advice could be sought from national

organisations, while the local authority contracted to provide some
of the funds.

Developing a resource inventory

The new policy of a mixed economy of care means that many more
services will be provided by the independent sector. To make this
work, the local authority must not merely define what services it is
looking for, but to do so with appropriate publicity, including both
formal advertisements and circulars (translated into appropriate
languages) and informal networks. In a survey of 11 London
boroughs, the lack of a thorough resource inventory was identified as
one common defect in the initial Community Care Plans.[10] The
information needed includes the department's own facilities, major
voluntary organisations identified in the community care plan, and
minor potential suppliers such as local voluntary groups. The
detailed work is best done at local level. A good starting point is to
mark up a large-scale map with coloured stickers, though there
should also be a more permanent record in the form of a resource file
or computer data base (the library service may help with this).
'Resources' at the local level include schools, shops, transport, pubs,
post offices, churches, parks and leisure centres — all the normal
facilities of daily life. Go for a walk and find out what's available and
where the gaps are. You can talk to people and find out what
resources they use and what more they would like. It is easy enough
to record social service facilities and the voluntary projects which
hold contracts with the council, but there may be many other small
voluntary groups — ask around among fellow professionals and
community contacts. This sort of information has to be constantly
updated, but when you issue a guide to resources, you can ask for
comments and additional information through a tear-off slip or a
telephone hotline.

Assessment of suppliers

The resource inventory gives a list of possible suppliers, but it won't
say how good they are. To get some idea of quality, ask questions
locally, and go and visit them all. The next stage is a more formal
evaluation, in terms of professional standards, management competence and financial viability, leading on to negotiation on contracts.
The process will involve various sections of the Social Services
department, but the initial checking out of professional practice may
be best done by local workers, who are on the look-out for resources
to meet specific needs, and for the possibility of working in
partnership with local agencies. The team can identify agencies with

potential, and help them to improve through giving advice or
offering training in subjects such as management or finance. There is
still a need for community development work — for example
through appointing planning officers for ethnic minority communities. At central level, it is important to continue to fund organisations that provide advice and training, like Councils of Voluntary
Service.

3.3   Marketing for providers of services

Providers of services — whether they are charities or privately
owned, are now in the same position as any other supplier — they
have to market and sell, or die. There is a problem of adjustment for
long-established suppliers, like some major charities, who used to
expect grants to be renewed more or less as a matter of course. There
is equally an opportunity for newcomers who have ideas and
expertise — provided they are aware of the hazards.

The marketing process

Marketing and selling is a cycle that can be divided into seven stages:

1. Decide what business you're in.
2. Find out what customers want.
3. Identify your unique advantage — what you can do that other
people can't.
4. Develop products and work out costs.
5. Make yourself and your products known.
6. Sell them.
7. Review the results; modify products, adjust your range and
sell elsewhere.

What business are you in?

   In practice any supplier will start part-way through this process.
Either they are selling to social service departments already (e.g. as
providers of residential homes), or they are starting up with a range
of skills and experience at their disposal. But even with this as a
guide, it is still crucial to decide on the limits of your business —
what work you will take and what you won't. One hazard is
expanding into business you don't really understand, or you are not
equipped to finance. Suppose a mental health project was a highly
successful provider of day care and drop-in services. As a natural
extension of this it might decide to set up a small residential home,

and go so far as to buy a house. At this stage it could find that planning consent, although informally promised, was refused and be left with a property it could neither use nor sell. But the opposite can be just as dangerous — looking on your skills too narrowly, so that you miss the real opportunities for expansion. In a service business, it is important that limits should be set coolly, and in advance: otherwise it is easy to say when talking to a customer 'We could certainly do that for you', and find yourself pitched into a new business by accident.

Who are the customers and what do they want?

Your customer, let us assume, is the local social service department. However it is an uncomfortable position to be tied to one customer, however benign (see below), and it is highly desirable to have others in mind — whether neighbouring authorities, voluntary organisations or private sector work of some sort.

News of opportunities will probably come through personal contacts — indeed if you have a strong connection with the local service department, much of your fact-finding will be done through the grapevine. However if you want to expand, you will have to approach some customers cold, and there is a good deal of research that can be done first, starting with the published policy statements of the local authority. From this you can discover their main priorities, and how satisfied they are with what is happening already. Other sources of information are the local paper, local community groups, and local and national charities. They may be your competitors in some fields, but they may still be prepared to exchange information or gossip. What you are trying to find out is:

(i) Who in the local authority is the person to talk to — the budget holder or purchaser? Who has the actual power to decide on (a) local interpretations of policy, and (b) awarding individual contracts? It may be useful to have contacts at member level; in some authorities the line between members and officers in decision-taking is somewhat blurred.

(ii) What are they buying-in now? How satisfied are they? What are they considering buying?

(iii) Your competitors — strengths and weaknesses.

(iv) Other products people are selling elsewhere — ideas you can adopt or adapt.

(v) Financial information — what the customer will pay.

From this information, you can build up a picture of what you have to offer before approaching the customer.

Making yourself known

A seller has to make their products and their expertise known. The main way of doing this is through personal contact, through public relations generally, or through literature such as brochures. (For discussion of public relations see chapter 7). Personal contacts have been discussed. Other means of publicity are local press and radio, which are usually hungry both for news and comment. If you have a success that can be made newsworthy, tell them: get to meet editors or reporters, and be in a position to ring them up. Other sources of publicity are professional press (writing articles etc.) or meetings of professional or community bodies, where you can find opportunities to speak. People with a professional background are not always good at blowing their own trumpet, or that of their organisation, but there is no one else to do it for them. The image to project is one that is professional, caring, and competent.

Be ready to share information informally with other agencies, unless they are head-on competitors (they can probably find out anyway).

An important source of publicity is your brochure. It should be designed and produced to be professional but not flashy (desk-top publishing is cheap), and should contain:

(i) What the organisation is — private or charitable status, how it is controlled etc.

(ii) Its philosophy — 'what we believe'.

(iii) The services on offer (in detail), together with the benefits — 'What we can do that other suppliers can't'.

(iv) Forms of agreement used.

(v) Organisation structure and staffing: membership of the Managing Council, or advisory bodies.

(vi) The system of contacts with clients — local authorities, carers and users; procedure for complaints or suggestions.

(vii) Charges and financial arrangements.

Developing a product and selling

● It can be hard to sell a product ready-developed: the alternative is to develop the product in partnership with social services. The best basis is a dialogue — professional to professional.

● The first step is to pinpoint the person who controls the budget, and convince them it's worth their while to talk to you. You may be able to use personal contacts — for example Social Services Inspectorate (SSI), or local community care forums or planning teams. You may have to sell on two levels — once to the person who decides that you are worth using, and once to whoever commissions the particular piece of work.

• At a meeting, your task is to listen and find out what they want. Then describe how you supply it, and point out your special strengths. Distinguish between old customers to whom you sell on your record, and new customers, who may need hyperbole.

• Sell your own unique strengths — what you do better than the competition, including the authority's own providing departments. Your likely advantages are cheapness, and/or quality. Because of local authorities' overheads, any independent supplier should be able to provide the same service at less cost — provided the local authority has got its costings right. You may also be able to sell on quality — offering something the authority simply can't provide. For example, an independent fostering service might offer a package of extra support for a child who requires exceptional care — a carer with professional nursing experience, backed up by transport and support during the day: in effect creating a full residential service in a domestic environment. Obviously services like this are only needed for a minority of cases, but once you become known as a reliable resource, mainstream work may develop.

• You may still need to educate people that times have changed and it is all right to use outside suppliers. Most departments are used to the idea of a mixed economy in community care, having used private residential homes for years, but children's services are some way behind, and you may need to show that there are no more protected patches for in-house providers.

The unequal bargain, and tendering

For providers of care, especially in rural areas, the local authority may be the only customer. This is an uncomfortable position for the supplier, and a potentially corrupting one for the authority: not so much financial corruption (though this is a possibility) but the corruption of too much power. If the authority is short of funds it will be tempted to squeeze suppliers beyond the point where they can stay in business: one authority recently decreed a 10 per cent cut in prices, and tried to impose it even on existing contracts. Tactics like this may be legitimate when relationships have got too easy, and prices are too high — though this would certainly suggest that the authority had been incompetent in the past. In many cases however, the better suppliers may go out of business, while the worse ones skimp on quality. There may also be a tendency for authorities to prefer to deal with minor local suppliers whom they can bully, rather than with national charities. If so, the independent market will not function as a pool of talent or a source of ideas. Suppliers may well be involved in competitive tendering. Tendering is a way of doing business that looks fair, and keeps down costs: it discourages the sort of cosy relationship where chosen suppliers get all the work, and charge over the odds for it. However tendering has its disadvantages — not least cost. For a fairly standard piece of work, a tender may involve no more work than writing a letter supported by a brochure, but tenders are apt to involve special requirements, and the cost of preparing the tender may be a serious part of the total cost. Moreover since for every tender suppliers win, they may have to tender several times unsuccessfully, to stay profitable they need to load the cost of all these other tenders onto their price. It is a temptation to under-cost a tender (you need the work, you have overheads to cover) — and then find that if you get the job it doesn't pay. On the other hand, one or other of your rivals may well shave their costs, so that if you charge a profitable rate, you simply miss it. In a buyers' market, an offer to tender can be a poison pill. There are also disadvantages to the purchaser: some suppliers may be driven out of business, others may refuse to tender and look for other work, or load their bid, on the outside chance that they may get it. The buyer needs a common sense approach: putting big jobs and long jobs out to tender, being prepared to change suppliers periodically, but awarding minor contracts on a fixed price basis to people who have their confidence.

Charities are considered here primarily in their role as suppliers. Often they have two other roles:

1. As providers of free or subsidised services which are paid for by their own fundraising.
2. As lobbyist for the interests of the people they are intended to benefit.

The first of these activities may be independent of work for local government, and shouldn't clash with it. In this role charities have the same problems of assessing need as local authorities, though their independent status may allow them to be pioneers, coping with needs that local authorities ignore. The second activity may be more problematic: if the aim of a charity is to promote the welfare of (say) old people, one of the things it may have to do is to scold local authorities that treat old people in ways the charity regards as niggardly or incompetent. Clearly the body you denounce in the morning may not be too keen to give you a contract in the afternoon, and charities may have to choose between their roles of watchdog and provider. In practice there may not be all that much difference between charitable and commercial status. True a charity has to plough any profits it makes back into the business, but so, in practice, will most commercial suppliers (both kinds of body will reward their staff if profits are high). In each case the main aims are likely to be the same — to satisfy the customer, while making enough income to pay the wages and stay in business. The managers of each sort of organisation are likely to have a similiar (often professional) background and outlook. It is not unusual for a body that started as a private company to turn itself into a charity, and carry on doing exactly the same job. One reason is that charities have certain legal rights that private companies don't, but a more general reason is that social service departments are more inclined to trust a charity than a private firm — so the decision is a marketing one.

Notes

1   Drucker, P.F. (1967) *Managing for Results*.
2   Taken from Juliet Cheetham 'Bridging the gaps in Community Care' *Community Care* June 24, 1991.
3   Originally proposed by Bradshaw, J. in 'The concept of human need' *New Society* March 30, 1972.
4   Doyal, I., Gough, I. (1991) *A Theory of Human Need*.
5   Curnock, K., Hardiker, P. (1070) *Towards Practice Theory, Skills and Methods in Social Assessment*.
6   Southwark Social Services Draft Community Care Plan 1993/94.
7   Percy-Smith, J., Sanderson, I. (1992) *Understanding Local Needs*.
8   Glampson, A., Scott, T., Thomas, D. (1975) *A Guide to the Assessment of Community Needs and Resources*.
9   Miller, C., Crosbie, D., Vickery, A. (1991) *Everyday Community Care: a manual for managers*.
10   Windle, K., Kerslake, A., Wright, J., Berry, S. (1992) *Capital Care Management*.

4 Costs, budgets and contracts

4.1 Controlling costs

If there is one thing certain about social work, it is that there will never be enough money to go round. Demand, through the raising of assumptions and standards of care, is infinite: resources are finite, in terms of what a society is prepared to spend, or can spend without substituting decline for growth. One can make a good case for saying that we spend much less on care than we should do: one cannot reasonably argue that spending should ignore cost and take account only of need. If resources are finite, it follows that they have got to be husbanded — getting value for money is as important to the relief of suffering as the provision of care itself, since it creates new resources that would otherwise be wasted.

To get value for money within an organisation, three things are needed:

1. The people who incur expenses should be committed to controlling costs.
2. People must know what costs are — both the costs of what they do now, and of alternative approaches.
3. Quality must be maintained.

These points are discussed below.

1. The people who incur expenses should be committed to controlling costs. Ideally, they should have a direct interest in keeping

them low. On a small fishing vessel, there may be no wages paid, but
the crew simply get half the profits: where this happens, not a ball of
twine gets lost overboard. This sort of arrangement is only possible
in small organisations run for profit. Larger, and non-profit making
organisations have to get the same effect by weaker means, such as
budgeting. This brings us to the second requirement.

2.   People must know what the costs are — both the costs of what
they do now, and of alternative approaches. This is not as easy as it
sounds. Consider even a simple operation in costing terms —
running an in-house residential home. Costs will be of four main
sorts:

- **Fixed costs** — those that go on being paid, even if there are
  no residents at all. The most obvious expense is rent — the
  building will always be there. Of course most local authorities own their property and don't pay rent. However if the
  money is tied up in owning a residential home, it can't be
  used elsewhere, or invested to give a cash return. Therefore
  the home still has to be charged for the value of the capital it
  uses — 'rent' under another name: otherwise the council will
  never know what the home is costing it in terms of benefits
  forgone. What this charge should be is not easy to estimate
  — it should really relate to the best alternative use of the
  money. Accountants have to follow some reasonable convention, and in this case the Treasury lays down a standard rate
  of interest for the public-sector.
- **Semi-variable costs.** Those you can change over a period,
  but not in response to short-term reductions in business.
  Staff costs are an example: if you know the home is going to
  be closed for rebuilding for eighteen months you can lay staff
  off, but not because of short-term changes of occupancy.
- **Variable costs.** These — like food and laundry — simply
  reflect the number of users.
- **Overheads** — the cost of supervising and administering the
  home, including its share of the cost of senior management,
  and of the inspection, personnel and accountancy functions.
  Leave these costs out, and it is impossible to make a fair
  comparison with the cost of going to an outside provider.
  However these costs can't possibly be 'accurate' — no one
  knows what proportion of her time the director spends
  pondering on the problems of residential homes generally,
  and 'Sunnybank' in particular. Once again, some common
  sense allocation has to be made.

One can see therefore that costing is largely a matter of judgement. Even in looking at costs for last year, there is scope for argument over the cost of capital and the allocation of overheads, as well as what should be set aside for repairs and maintenance — perhaps nothing at all was spent last year, but taking one year with another the costs could be high. When it comes to estimating costs in the future — particularly the cost of accommodating one inmate for a week, uncertainties are far greater. The only thing you are certain of is the variable costs — e.g. food: any other cost depends on how full the home will be. If it is half empty, fixed costs and overheads *per user* will more or less double, and staff costs per user will go up by a rather smaller amount (depending on how far you can save staff). At the end of the day, all accounting, especially drawing up budgets, depends heavily on assumptions and common sense, and managers should take some interest in how sensible accountants' assumptions actually are.

The third need in getting value for money is maintaining quality. In some trades this is not all that difficult — if quality drops, customers grumble or disappear. In social work, the customer (the local authority) is not in fact the user, and the user has no alternative to go to, which makes quality control a severe challenge — see chapter 5.

4.2 Budgets and their uses

A budget is a detailed estimate of receipts and expenditure over some future period. Budgets can be used in one of three ways:

- As a forecast, on which plans can be based. 'We expect to feed twice as many people at the luncheon club next year, so we must budget for expanding the kitchen, and paying two more cooks'.
- As a target. 'Your job is to make sure that fees from counselling double next year'.
- As a constraint. 'You can spend up to £10,000, and then you stop'.

Since budgets include the whole range of financial factors, it will often happen that some of the figures are forecasts, being right out of the control of the unit being budgeted for (like it or not, these are your overheads), other figures are targets, and others again are absolute restraints. Many of these figures are interdependent. If you are drawing up a budget for a residential home, the expected (or target) occupancy level is essential data for estimating food and other variable costs. Sometimes you may work out several trial budgets, based on different assumptions — 'Let's assume occupancy at 60 per cent, and see what that does to costs.' The process of drawing up budgets usually consists of sitting down with last year's figures, thinking about what is likely to change, and inserting new figures. Usually an organisation will require the same basic assumptions to be used by all its departments ('rates of pay are expected to rise by 5 per cent').

As a way of getting value for money, budgets have one grave flaw — that a manager's apparent success depends heavily on her ability to manipulate the system. The art is to get your budget as high as possible, and spend every penny — otherwise it may be cut next year. A great deal of misplaced skill goes into exaggerating probable costs, so that if they turn out to be less, you get the credit for making savings. Compare the situation where suppliers are independent, and there is a ready market. Here the purchaser knows exactly what each item costs — it costs whatever the supplier charges. If there is proper competition, suppliers will not want to be undersold, but will set their prices at a level that will just bring in an acceptable profit. If the risk is high, the profit required will be higher — suppliers have to insure themselves against the chance of making a loss. On occasion, the cost the supplier charges may have no relation to average costs. Suppose he has a residential home, on the border of two authorities. He sells 80 per cent of his bed-space to one authority, and this is enough to cover his costs. It may then be worth his while to offer the other authority his spare bed-space very cheaply — his fixed costs are covered, and any extra revenue (less variable costs) is pure profit. Alternatively, he may have a full house, and if the authority asks him to accommodate more people, he may quote a very high charge — extra users will involve building extra rooms, so the immediate cost may be very high, and he may not care if the authority takes its extra business elsewhere. Of course suppliers themselves have to budget carefully to make sure they are profitable (see 4.5), but for the purchaser, the transaction is far simpler.

Sometimes you find a mixed situation: under the authority's contract, the supplier is only allowed a small profit, and anything extra gets clawed back by the authority. A system like this may make sense while both sides are finding their feet, but in the long term it is foolish, since the purchaser is faced with having to audit all the supplier's costs, while the supplier has no incentive to improve efficiency.

4.3 Devolving budgets

A large organisation can either keep control of its budgets centrally, or it can pass some or all of the decisions down the line. To take the simplest example of a supplier unit, like an in-house residential home, the control systems, in order of devolution, might be as follows.

1. The budget is wholly centralised: all expenditure is approved in advance with Head Office, who will add up the costs and pay the bills. Staffing and wages are decided centrally.

2. The local manager is given a small sum to spend on minor items: she keeps a record plus receipts, which are checked periodically.

3. The local manager is given a budget to spend under various headings (food, cleaning materials, laundry etc.): she may or may not be allowed to spend more on one item and less on another. Bills are paid and detailed records kept at Head Office.

4. The local manager is given a budget for staff costs and given discretion to make changes, such as two part-timers for one full-timer: hourly rates may still be decided or negotiated centrally.

5. The manager is given a total budget, related to the number of inmates, to spend at discretion.

The more the budget is devolved, the more chance the local manager has to make mistakes or even act dishonestly — these are the inevitable penalties of allowing discretion. At the same time, the better the chance of getting value for money. If the local manager knows a jobbing builder who can fix the roof tomorrow, the work may be done far sooner and at a fraction of the cost. The manager may or may not have an interest in getting value for money: at one extreme, she may not get any cost information at all; at the other extreme she could be paid a commission on cost savings, giving her much the same incentives as an outside supplier. In the first case, senior management must concentrate on seeing that costs are kept down: in the second, it will be more concerned with quality — making sure the local manager is not skimping on either service to users or maintenance. There is no right solution on how far to devolve, since it depends partly on how capable, caring and honest managers are. Responsibility for budgets should match the responsibility devolved to managers in other areas: it is sometimes found that managers are allowed vast discretion in operational decisions, but are still not allowed to spend a penny on their own authority.

Devolving budgets to providers is relatively straightforward, since their costs can be forecast quite accurately. Devolving budgets to care managers is more complex. The principle is the same — if managers have a budget to spend on clients, and discretion on how they spend it, they will tend to get better value for money — for example, by arranging to keep people in their own homes. It may not be too difficult to set a budget for an existing case-load, but it is far harder to assess the costs of new clients. If budgets are devolved to individual case managers, any one of them could be faced with a quite unforeseeable increase in costs and run out of money in the first six months, while another is flush with unspent funds (this has been a problem in the health service). To make devolution work, some compromises are necessary, such as:

1. Devolving budgets to areas, and no further;
2. Keeping a large contingency reserve that senior managers can allocate for unexpected needs;
3. Calculating a standard budget for each category of need, or devising a points system.

At present devolution is being extended very fast, and appropriate systems will no doubt soon get established.

4.4 Budgetary information

No budget system can work, unless the budget-holder has the right information. Setting up information systems was one of the Key Tasks (Task 6) that authorities were meant to carry out prior to implementation of the NHS and Community Care Act in April 1993, but some made more progress than others. In care management, the information needed by budget-holders is of two main sorts:

1. Client data   — Records for current clients
                  — Referral and assessment data
                  — Packages of care management in operation
                  — Expected number of hospital discharges
                  — Demographic data for forward planning.
2. Financial data — Amounts budgeted under each heading
                  — How much has been spent in each period
                  — Orders in the pipeline.

This information needs to be regular and up-to-date, and the financial and quantitative data have to tie up. An additional problem is that not many accounts systems can yet provide the necessary financial information centrally, so that budget-holders may have to keep their own private records, which means there is yet a third lot of data to be reconciled. Since two sets of financial records never in practice agree, there is ample scope for overspending and argument. (Apart from simple adding mistakes, the most common source of disagreement is attributing an item of expenditure to the wrong period.) If information can't be produced centrally, it is better to give budget-holders a standardised system for keeping memorandum accounts. There are several computer packages newly on the market, which may or may not suit the needs of a particular authority. On the other hand the simplest system is often the best — a set of pigeon holes for orders, plus an old-fashioned add-listing machine, may take less time and be easier to reconcile.

4.5 Budgeting and planning for providers

Budgeting is at least as important for an independent supplier as it is for a local authority. Local authorities can be capped: independent suppliers can go bust. The manager of any business needs an adequate set of financial records — enough to be sure (a) that money will come in in time to pay the debts, and (b) that the business is making a profit. These records must be capable of being extended into the future, via the budgetary system: the company must be able to estimate its financial position for at least a year ahead, taking account of down-risks such as losing customers.

The financial system must also be good enough to provide the detailed information on the basis of which decisions can be taken. If the intention is to bid for a contract, what price should be asked? In the case of a straightforward business having only one product, like a residential home, management must:

— Estimate fixed costs, variable costs, overheads and capital expenditure for the duration of the contract
— Estimate how many units of care it will supply (for a residential home, a unit of care might be one bed for one week)
— Divide its total cost by the number of units, and fix the price of one unit accordingly (adding on a margin for accidents, and for profit).

With something like a drug project, the problem is greater: 'Products' may range from a bed in a residential treatment unit, to counselling sessions, or drop-in facilities, and costs have to be worked out for each of them if proper charges are to be made (this matters most when an independent supplier is providing different services to different authorities).

In drawing up budgets and making tenders, charities have certain problems to be wary of. The first is the relationship between their charitable income (donations and so on) and their trading income. For a start, their position in terms of tax and VAT needs to be looked at with care. Then they must ask themselves whether the donors would approve of their gifts being used to help the charity bid for a contract. If, for example, donations cover their overheads, is it ethical for them to use this advantage to underbid rivals who happen to be private suppliers? The same thing applies to the work of volunteers. To get a true picture of costs, charities should estimate the cost of work done by a volunteer at the price they would have to pay a professional to do it. Otherwise they may be in trouble if a valuable volunteer suddenly disappears, while the volunteers themselves may not be happy if their freely given time is in effect merely reducing the price paid for services by the local council.

Financial information is one element in drawing up a business plan. The purpose of this is to pull together the information that any manager should have at his fingertips (though many don't): what the business is going to do to make a profit and pay its bills, what its activities will be, and where the money will come from. (For in-house suppliers, the equivalent document is the Service Plan.) Documents like this are dear to the heart of bank managers when they are asked for a loan, since they want some assurance that they will get their money back. Where a long-term contract is in question, purchasers may want to ask similar questions: they need to be assured that the supplier's business is adequately run, capable of doing what it says it will in a competent and caring manner, and likely to stay in business for the contract's duration. They need to know that capital expenditure will be covered, together with start-up expenses such as training.

There may be a problem in giving a purchaser too much information of this sort: after all if they know the supplier's likely profit, they can use the information in negotiating to squeeze prices. Where sensitive information is called for, the supplier should propose, and the purchaser accept, that it should be given in confidence to someone from a different department within the authority (such as the Treasurer's), and not be disclosed to whoever is negotiating the contract.

Information that may be contained in a business plan includes the following.

1. The aims of the organisation:
   - Values, strategy and main business
   - Services it provides to clients
   - Premises, and other major assets

2. Direction and management:
   - Names of board and managers, their background and experience
   - Other sources of expertise
   - How the business is controlled and run
   - Management systems and sources of management information

- Contingencies, and how they will be dealt with

3. Financial information:
   - Latest results, projections for the future, and assumptions on which they are made.
   - Financial systems: enough detail to know that management will be able to keep control of costs and cash flow.

4. Policies and major plans:
   - Business in hand or expected; sources of new business
   - Staff policies — training, recruitment, participation
   - Equal opportunities
   - Mechanisms for consultation and complaints.

4.6   Creating a market

(How far an authority wishes to contract-out services is a political decision. This section is written for those that do.)
   The benefits of going to outside suppliers should be:

1. Increasing efficiency and innovation through competition
2. Establishing the true costs of care
3. Reducing costs, by putting provision of services on a less bureaucratic basis.

Without competition, aims 1. and 2. won't work, while bureaucratic controls will have to be re-introduced to prevent monopoly suppliers from exploiting their position. Hence the importance of establishing a lively market in care services. At present, even where councils are enthusiastically trying to contract out, a market hardly exists. Judging by the 1992 study 'Contracting for Care',[1] nearly all contracting out is to suppliers already well known to the social services departments — in some cases to ex-members of staff, in others to national charities. As things stand, departments have little choice, and faced as they are with a severe reduction in their direct control of the care process, they are not surprisingly going to people they know. However giving business to old friends can slide imperceptibly from quality control to corruption, and authorities should see it as a duty to offer work to a range of suppliers where they exist, and where they don't, to encourage people to set up in business.
   The most important step is publicity. Councils should advertise the sorts of services they may need, the standards they require, and the means they employ for purchasing, using both formal advertise-

ments and circulars (translated into appropriate languages) and informal networks. A study carried out in Wiltshire concluded that 'Voluntary Organisations would have welcomed information to help them to see how their work fits in with Social Services'.[2] It is also important to give guidance on timing: it may take a potential supplier six months or more to put together an operation that can seriously contract for work. Obvious potential suppliers are former social services or health services staff, qualifying students, people with a hotel and catering background (for residential services), and for particular projects people with a legal, trade union, or industrial welfare background. One crucial source is community groups, who may be the best people to provide services that will suit clients who are also their neighbours. It is worthwhile fostering groups like these, and being prepared to offer training — though avoiding favouritism, in what has got to be an arms-length transaction if a market is to be established.

Another important consideration is to be prepared to talk to people, whether they come to make enquiries or sell an idea. One of the temptations of power — including purchasing power — is to rebuff people who approach you. In this case even rather ignorant or inept salesmen are doing you a service, if they provide an alternative to a monopoly.

4.7 Contracting

A contract here is an agreement with a supplier to provide services. Not all supplies will be under contract — authorities will still subsidise some kinds of organisation by grant. There is, after all, no point in having a contract with a community group to which you give a few hundred pounds a year — if they don't do what you expect of them, you can simply stop their grant. In cases of Service agreements for tasks of any size, however, we can expect contracts to take over, whether these are formal contracts, or service level agreements.

The starting point for a contract should be the **Service Specification**. This is the formal statement of what the authority intends to provide, and the bridge between assessment of need and the actual provision of services. It is therefore essential to draw one up for any service the authority provides, whether or not it is to be contracted out. It should include:

— The aims of the service, in the light of identified needs and the policy of the department;
— What the service consists of in detail, including staffing and training

- The intended results, and numbers of people
- Quality standards
- Arrangements for monitoring and inspection.

(The service agreement is also the basis of service plans for individual users, which set out exactly what each individual can expect.)

Block and spot contracts

A contract may be for a number of services over a period — a 'block contract', or for one individual — a 'spot contract'. The advantage of block contracts is that suppliers have work guaranteed for a period (typically three years), and so can budget on a level of occupancy and set prices accordingly. The disadvantage is that the choice of the authority is limited for that period: it can't shift its business if it finds a better source of supply, and it can't offer its clients choice — unless it has several contracts for the same service. Where there is a block contract, budget-holders will normally be required to use the contracted facilities, which may have to be paid for in any case. Spot contracting is more usual for dealing with special cases requiring complex care.

What should a contract contain?

Since a contract is legally enforceable, lawyers (on both sides) will need to read it through. It is a matter of judgement whether lawyers should draw it up in full legalistic form. Some authorities have made long-term agreements on the basis of a simple exchange of letters (or even through word-of-mouth arrangements, which is certainly risky). Suppliers who have a close relationship with social services departments say that they expect to be treated as professionals — you don't need a detailed contract with your doctor or architect. With a short-term contract, there is not much problem — in cases of dispute the authority can refuse to renew it, or use the threat to put pressure on the supplier. On the other hand, the authority has a statutory duty towards its clients, and it might conceivably find itself being sued by them if the contractor failed to deliver. Certainly the Association of Metropolitan Authorities[3] takes a cautious view, and recommends a fully detailed contract, including performance bonds that can be forfeited for poor standards. This has the advantage that the authority can put pressure on the supplier to improve without having to terminate the contract, though with some kinds of service it may not be possible to specify standards in enough detail. An alternative might be a clause providing for arbitration, possibly backed up by a system of independent inspection (itself contracted out).

Even if a contract is informal or by letter, the least it should specify is:

- The service to be provided, and major elements of quality — e.g. the proportion of qualified workers to be employed.
- The number of users, and any restrictions on the sort of people accepted (some schemes might not accept users with a record of violence)
- Duration of contract, and procedure for varying it
- The procedure if anything goes wrong — complaints, investigation, arbitration etc.
- Charges and financial arrangements. It is important to specify all costs at the outset, to prevent unexpected charges for extras. It is equally important to make sure that the arrangements encourage the supplier to reduce costs. On some contracts, the authority pays the cost of the service, and adds on a 15 per cent management charge: with this arrangement, the supplier actually has an incentive to keep costs high. Any cost-plus contract should allow the supplier to keep a proportion of any savings, both as an incentive, and to provide a fund for development. One authority at least is trying to tie payment to performance, based on indicators such as cleanliness, food quality, number of staff employed, signs of customer happiness etc. Certainly independent inspection is needed for this system to work.

Some suppliers have standard agreements (to which modifications could be negotiated), or else have brochures or policy statements that can be referred to in the contract as a way of establishing standards. Authorities themselves will have statements of requirements for suppliers.

4.6   Commissioning

When the Authority has decided what work it wants done, the next stage is to choose a provider. The most obviously fair way to do this is by tender. However tendering is a time-consuming and expensive process, especially for suppliers, and the cost of a failed tender is never recouped. As a result, tenderers have to put up their prices substantially — for a small contract, sometimes by as much as 40 or 50 per cent. Tendering is not mandatory for social service departments, but it may be worthwhile for a big contract, where there is competition. If so, an Invitation to Tender should be prepared, specifying:

- The aims of the contract: who is contracting, what they want done, and when.
- Detailed objectives and quality standards
- Resources the supplier must have
- Financial arrangements
- Arrangements for submitting bids, and the process of choosing — presentations etc. It is in fact illegal for the authority to accept bids outside the stated time.
- Who is handling the contract, and can be contacted.

Where tendering is not used, authorities should still be transparent and fair in their choice, making it known who decides, and by what criteria. It may be reasonable to give some preference to people you know well and have worked with before: if so, you should say so frankly, but give new proposers a chance to show their credentials — e.g. by being prepared to discuss their record with other authorities who have used them. You may feel you know your local market but it may be worth advertising the contract to see if anyone better comes up. In urban areas there may well be suppliers who deal with neighbouring boroughs with whom you have not yet had any contact. Where you have a choice, cheapness will certainly be one criterion, but it is even more important to ask whether the supplier is efficient, honest, caring and financially sound.

Tendering for suppliers

The first question for a supplier is whether to bid at all. Is the work within your scope, can you handle the volume, and have you a reasonable chance of getting the contract? If the answer to all these is yes, you have the job of preparing a bid, which can be onerous. You may already know quite a lot about the job, having talked to the Department beforehand, or you may be in a position to talk to them now. In either case your first guide should be the tender document — read it with empathy to decide what they really want. Then extract from your business plan the parts that show that you can fulfil it.

In deciding what price you will bid, be aware that the main temptation is to ask too little. Make sure you build in:

- Enough to clear direct costs and overheads and make an acceptable surplus
- Provision for inflation, if the contract is for more than a year

- Provision for down-risks and contingencies, including low numbers of clients. Consider too the effect of any penalty clause.
- The cost of preparing your bid (allowing for the fact that you may have to bid for several contracts before you are successful). Of course if you add all these in, you may lose the contract. In some cases you may choose to take the job at a loss to establish yourself with the authority, but be clear that too many loss leaders is the surest way to bankruptcy.

Contract management and compliance

Once the contract has been signed, both sides need to keep it going. Any contract involving a long-term supply of services should be a partnership: it is in the interest of both sides for contacts to be frequent and informal, to make life easier for each other, and to accept minor variations of performance. It is not however in the interests of the purchaser to allow standards to slip overall.

There should usually be one designated person who handles transactions under the contract, acts as point of contact, passes on inspection and monitoring reports, and negotiates plans for improvement. It is best if this person really understands the service being provided — a contract for child care should be managed by a child care worker. Under a flexible system of management (see chapter 9), a block contract for the whole department could be managed by someone from within an area team. The contract manager should always be supervised by someone more senior: it is all very well establishing close relations with suppliers, but they can get too close.

The supplier may have greater problems. A large long-term contract may involve expanding the organisation, creating new units, and promoting new managers. Setting up the contract needs rather different skills from maintaining it — which requires skills of routine, of listening to users, making best use of monitoring, and building-up trust.

Negotiation

The principles of negotiation are very much the same, whether the issue is between a commissioning authority and supplier, a social worker and client, or conflicting public agencies. Negotiation is essentially the process of reconciling aims. In the most basic transaction, the buyer wants goods, the seller wants money, and negotiation is simply about how much. In more complicated situations, the two sides want results which appear to be incompatible, and negotiation is the process of exploring ways in which both of them can be satisfied. A social worker may want a psychiatric patient to be rehabilitated in a therapeutic hostel: the patient may adamantly refuse. The outcome of negotiation might be that the patient moves into a flat with a friend, and attends a mental health day centre. Here both sides achieve their fundamental aims — the social worker, that the patient is supported and kept occupied, the patient, he avoids being stuck in yet another institution. In social work it is quite rare for either side to get exactly what they want: it is almost always better to have an agreement that both sides can accept, rather than an imposed solution which the client will always fight against. A solution like this will never come about through sterile haggling, but only when both sides join forces to treat apparently conflicting aims as a problem for both of them.

Some guidelines for negotiation are:

1. Don't take up entrenched positions, or declare what you're insisting on; rather state your fundamental aims, and explore the aims of the other party.
2. Try to find a creative solution that suits both sides.
3. Avoid haggling: instead, try to find a rule or principle that both sides can accept — though making sure that the principle suits your argument. For a supplier negotiating with an authority, one principle might be: 'We work for three other boroughs, and none of them insists on this'; or 'Surely whoever makes the savings ought to keep the benefit?'; or 'This is what the Act obviously means'.
4. Know your own fall-back position — what else you can do if you can't get an agreement.
5. Keep the goodwill of the other party. If you have a threat up your sleeve, let them know of it, but don't try to bully them. The only time you may need to attack is if the other side are frivolously defending an untenable position, or refusing to face reality. In cases like this, good negotiators may attack with sudden and devastating force.
6. Don't drive such a hard bargain that the other party is crushed — you may well need to deal with them again.

The final point applies particularly to local authorities. They are often in an immensely strong position, being the only customer for some services. They shouldn't abuse this by driving such a hard bargain that there is nothing in it for the other party: if they do, supplies will simply dry up. Some authorities choose to deal with small local organisations, which are cheap (having no overheads), and which they can bully. Such behaviour is worse than criminal — it is short-sighted: if the private and voluntary sectors are to continue their record of innovation, developing new services, and training staff, there must be a reasonable allowance for overheads and profit.

Notes

1. Common and Flynn (1992).
2. Meadows (1992).
3. Association of Metropolitan Authorities (1991).

5 Quality assurance

5.1 Some definitions

The language of quality is confusing, so it may be useful to start by defining how various terms are used in this chapter.

- **Quality** means 1. fitness for purpose; 2. degree of excellence (Oxford English Dictionary).
- **Quality assurance** means the attempt to ensure that services provided meet the standards set and the needs of the consumer, both now and in future. Quality assurance is therefore concerned with *aims*.
- **Quality control** means the system for evaluating the quality of services provided (or goods produced). With goods, quality control takes place in the factory, before the customer gets them: with services, quality control normally happens after delivery, though it provides information that helps quality assurance in the future.
- **Monitoring** means the routine collection of data on service delivery.
- **Evaluation** means using the data to assess how well services meet their stated aims.

5.2 Total Quality Management

Total Quality Management (TQM) is a catchphrase whose time has come, but it is also a valuable management idea. If it is to work, everyone in the organisation, including people at the very top, have to rethink the way they, personally, operate, and this means a heavy injection of training (see chapter 8). But even without this, the TQM concept can help the work of an individual department (though without top-level support, it will not be 'total'), and it is worth the individual manager understanding it. Independent providers of services are in a better position to put TQM in place. The section below is not a manual on how to do it, but an introduction to the idea.

The principle of TQM is straightforward — customers should be not merely satisfied, but actually 'delighted' with the services they receive. For this to happen, it is not enough to have good salesmen and efficient delivery: the product itself has to be excellent, which means that all stages of design, manufacture and sales have to observe the same high standards. It follows that the 'customers' who must be delighted include not merely external ones, but also internal ones — anyone who receives a service or is passed on a product from any other part of the organisation. In a factory, the assemblers should be delighted with the components they receive: in an office, letter-writers should be delighted with the products of the typing pool. Naturally standards must take account of the kind of product or service that is on offer: quality means fitness as well as excellence, and people buying a family car shouldn't expect a Rolls Royce — merely an extremely well-designed and well-built family car.

It is all very well to announce that you are going to delight your customers, but how do you set about it? You must obviously have a well-run organisation, and a skilful work-force — that applies to any successful organisation — but TQM makes some special demands:

1. Agreement between departments on what standards are looked for, and rapid feedback on how well they are achieved.
2. Documentation, both of standards and processes for achieving them. The documentation mustn't sit in an archive, but be a constant guide to the operators, and be regularly updated.
3. Readiness of departments to co-operate in improving standards.
4. The commitment of individual employees to seeing that standards are met.

This last is a tall order. In Britain we have rather a mixed tradition. In small organisations, people sometimes have a very high commitment to standards, and everyone works together to make sure they are met, but our talent for co-operation tends to desert us in larger units. A lot of British companies that tried to introduce TQM have failed, while those who succeeded did so by paying exceptional attention to the human issues — co-operation between departments, and the training and commitment of staff.

In social work TQM implies that at every point of interaction, the customer must be delighted: 'customer' must be understood in the widest sense — in a case conference, most of the parties are customers of each other. Some of the main interactions are shown on the diagram below (Fig. 5.1).

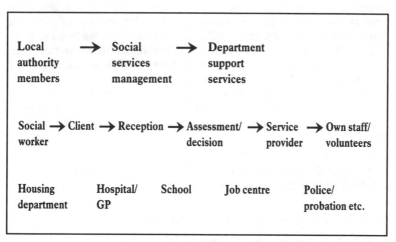

Figure 5.1

Every arrow shows at least a potential customer–supplier relationship. There are four main series of links where Quality Management needs to operate:

1. Within the local authority — the links between members, senior officers, support services, and social work staff.
2. The links between client, social workers, and suppliers of services.
3. The links between social workers and parallel organisations — housing, health, schools etc.
4. The links between service providers, and their own staff and volunteers.

In the first link-series, the main responsibility lies with senior officers, who are, after all, the professional managers, while the last series is mainly a matter for providers of services. In the other two series, much responsibility lies with individual social workers and first-line management. Setting and documenting standards is described in the next section (it is already well advanced in some authorities, particularly for relations between providers and clients).

What is needed to take the TQM concept further is to set standards for the relationship with other departments. Take the relationship between social services and the housing department — both part of the same organisation. At present, every case that needs re-housing tends to be a matter of negotiation, sapping the time and energy of both sides. It would be perfectly possible for the two sides to agree standards of what they expect, and guidelines they will follow, for all except the most exceptional cases. Social services is normally (though not invariably) the customer, and so has most to gain, which makes the negotiation more difficult, but both sides are likely to benefit. Education too is merely another department of the main authority, and the process could well be extended to other agencies such as health services and the police.

For what might be called 'Extended' — rather than 'Total' — Quality Management, the personal commitment of senior managers is not essential, but at least their passive benevolence will be needed. The stages are:

1. Identify the main links to be worked on, and get the agreement of 'customers' and 'suppliers' to try and improve co-operation.

2. Choose a link to start on, some criteria being:

   (a) Other parties involved are interested
   (b) There are recurrent transactions which cause serious (but not insuperable) problems for both sides.
   (c) Transactions are often handled by the same few people, who can take part in planning (you don't want a first trial that has to involve half the county).

3. Set up a meeting with other parties' representatives and analyse:

   (a) What form transactions take, and how they should be classified.
   (b) The aims of each transaction. In many cases, the aims of different bodies will be different (see chapter 2, page 30). If aims are complex use a Why/How network.
   (c) What are the strengths of the present system — what works smoothly and well (in making improvements, take care not to lose what you have got).
   (d) Problems, and their causes
   (e) Standards that should be aimed at (see next section)
   (f) Procedures that will achieve those standards
   (g) People not present whose agreement will be needed to make changes.

4. Document the standards and procedures — a job for individuals or pairs rather than a meeting.

5. Reconvene the meeting to discuss and approve them, and agree a trial run.

6. Arrange a trial, reviewing briefly after each transaction.

7. Review the trial as a whole, and amend standards and procedures.

8. Get support for a full-scale trial, and go-ahead.

Tackling quality in this way will improve both services and working lives, but it will involve a lot of effort in the short term, and the manager who gets it going will need both persuasiveness and vision. It is possible to work gradually — tackle a small area and get results, and then use this to get the support of senior management for larger attempts.

5.3 Setting standards

Quality depends on aims — both the aims of the client, and the aims of the authority. A high-quality service means that customers get what they want — and/or that the responsibilities of the authority are fulfilled. The starting point will be the various aims-related statements in the authority's plan, such as the Mission statement, Service Values, and Aims for each unit. From these the stages are:

1. Setting standards
2. Deriving performance indicators
3. Monitoring performance
4. Review and evaluation of results
5. Taking steps to improve performance: perhaps also a rethinking of aims and standards.

It may be useful to recall some of the definitions on page 28 (in chapter 2). In this section we are talking about **continuous tasks** (e.g. running a residential home) rather than tasks that can be completed, so the relevant kinds of standard relate to (1) The way the job is done (e.g. 'using qualified staff'); (2) The list of performance (e.g. 'meals are always hot'); (3) The results of the job (e.g. user satisfaction). Before you can monitor results, standards have to be supported by **indicators** — ways of judging whether the standard is being met: once again these may be **result indicators** or **performance indicators**. Finally most indicators have to be quantified, and turned into **measures** and the monitoring/inspection process can take the form of **sample tests**, of whether the measures are being achieved.

To give an example, in assessing residential accommodation, a standard stated by *Home Life* and the Wagner report is that elderly residents should continue to have access to community resources. The results standard is that residents feel in touch with local people rather than cut off from the community. The performance standard is the number and nature of the community contacts made by residents. Indicators might cover questioning residents about their most recent activities, as well as a map or chart of local contacts and records of outings or visits. Measures might include the number and range of contacts, and also a visual display of recent activities. Sample tests might include accompanying a resident on an outing or a regular visit.

Setting standards should be a collaborative process, involving all the interested parties; within an organisation, this means customers, both front line and support staff, and managers at two or three levels. Within the community care system it might include users, purchasers, providers, carers, other professionals and community groups. A good approach is to get together a working party containing members of all these groups: the combined membership should have direct experience of all the stages of service, from initial interview to completion. The mood of the meeting is crucial: it is important to encourage staff and suppliers, by giving full credit to what they have done already — even if users' representatives are arguing that they should be doing a great deal more. It is equally important to create an atmosphere in which users' views can be heard. The process should encourage everyone present to see themselves as part of a large-scale team, rather than as lone operators: it should reassert common values, and aim to dissipate suspicion.

5.4 Why/how network in setting standards

A good way of working is to use a why/how network, as described on page 30. A why/how network provides, first, a statement of the main aims being pursued, and how one aim contributes towards another; secondly, a statement of the main means, and the relationship between them. Its benefits are:

— comprehensiveness — the logic makes it harder to leave things out;
— Logical order — the relation between results standards and performance standards is made clear;
— Democracy — it allows large numbers of people to contribute, in a fairly short period.

The procedure is easy to follow, and anyone can contribute — though whoever runs the meeting will have to understand the method thoroughly. (If an outside facilitator can't be found, a dummy run with a couple of colleagues will reveal any snags.) The procedure is set out below, based on the example of standards for services for people with Aids or those who are HIV positive.

1. Equipment needed: masking tape, flip chart paper, sheets of A5-sized scrap paper, one thick felt-tipped pen for each person present, and a large blank wall.

2. Propose an opening statement to the meeting, on the lines of 'Run a high quality service for people with Aids/HIV' or whatever service you are working on. (The choice of statement is important, so test it with a colleague, to see that it engenders the sort of answers you expect.) Write the statement in felt tip on a slip of paper, and fix it with masking tape in the middle of the blank wall.

3. Pose the question 'Why provide services for people with Aids in Xton? Invite participants to print answers (purposes) in felt tip on single sheets of paper. Collect answers and fix them to the wall, above the opening statement. Group together statements dealing with similar issues, eliminating any that are exact duplicates.

4. Take the original statement, and other significant purposes, and ask How they are to be achieved — answers in felt tip as before. If many people are present, it may save time to invite sections of the meeting to concentrate on providing 'hows' for different parts of the network.

5. Pin up How answers, grouping them on the wall so as to provide a logical network. Again eliminate duplicates, but don't sacrifice ideas which look similar but have different shades of meaning.

6. Take each of the How answers, and ask again how each is to be achieved.

7. Check the network for completeness — it should show all the activities carried out now, together with their aims. It will also

probably show a number of things that aren't done. These are not relevant to the process of setting standards, but should be listed as possible new services. Explain that those that are expensive are unlikely to get very far, but some ideas may be cheap, or may be more effective substitutes for what is done now.

Take the boxes one by one, and ask 'how can we tell that the task is being carried out properly?' or 'What standard should we expect?' People may come up with standards or performance indicators. It might seem logical to ask for standards first, but most people are better at thinking in concrete terms, and may find it easier to think of an indicator or test: it is more natural for people to think in terms of 'people at work not knowing that I come here' (indicator) rather than 'ensuring confidentiality' (standard). If you have the indicators, you can work back to standards later. There is no need to burden non-professional participants with the distinction. Not every box will generate a standard — it may be more realistic to set a standard for a box higher or lower in the chain. If for example a section of a network reads as shown in Figure 5.2, one can see from this that the distinction between result indicators and performance indicators depends on which box you take as your task. The result of a lower level task, like 'be careful about what you say on the phone', is part of the performance of a higher level one, like 'ensure confidentiality'. On the whole it is easier to measure a lower-level box (the service provided), rather than a higher one, like the effect on the client. However this can be a snare — there is no point in having the best service in the world if the clients don't want it and a wise department will include some result indicators as a check.

If the meeting is a large one (ten or more members) or the network is complex, it may be best to divide into sub-groups, and give each a section of the network to handle. (Members of sub-groups should have experience of the services being worked on, but probably *not* include the manager directly responsible for the service, in case she inhibits discussion.) Ask for suggestions, and note them all (however daft or dismissive of social services) on a 'flip chart', or large sheet of paper pinned on the wall (using a broad felt-tipped pen, so everyone can read). Then try to get consensus on which of them would be most useful, in the sense of being (a) a good test of success, (b) objective, and (c) easily verified (if you can't get consensus, include minority views in the report-back). You can use standards from similar organisations as a check (or prompt), but don't disclose them all before the group has developed its own list. Sub-groups should then report back to the main meeting.

The final stage is to test the proposed criteria on existing services, and see, in the view of people present, how well they are met. You

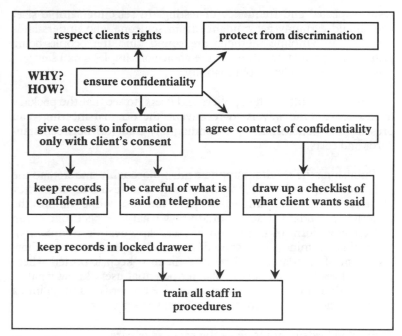

Figure 5.2

may get a wide sample of views, since answers may vary from team to team. Note the teams where high standards are found, so that in due course their successful practices can be identified and spread to others.

A representative meeting of this sort should provide the data needed for setting standards, but standards also depend on resources, and there may be a trade-off between quality and costs. Decisions are the responsibility of the authority, and it may be better for the work to be done by social services staff. The stages are:

1. Defining standards, in the light of priorities of need, current best practice, and resources available. It is sometimes useful to set standards at two levels — the bare minimum, and the standard regarded as satisfactory. Minimum standards should be such that a supplier who fails to meet them is replaced (contracts can provide for this).

2. Choosing indicators that in combination will provide a clear picture of whether standards are being met.

3. Deciding on tests, the form they should take, sample size, level of

result expected and frequency of testing. In selecting sample size, you should certainly get guidance from someone who understands statistics: if sampling methods are sound (and the people being tested can't predict or influence the choice of sample) small samples can often give high levels of reliability.

4. Checking results with suppliers and users, to see that the package makes sense. One way is to reconvene the original meeting, and present your conclusions — defending any trade-off between standards and costs.

5. Publishing the results. Suppliers must thoroughly understand the standards required, but not necessarily the tests, in case they contrive to rig the sample, or pass the test while failing the underlying standard. Users should know what to expect (one cheap and effective form of inspection is users' approval or complaints). With this in mind, you should provide suppliers with a short statement of standards, and require them to keep it posted where users can read it. You should also let potential users know what to expect well in advance: if a client is to give up her flat and go into a residential home, she needs to know what she's getting.

Some standards in practice — the process of care

The first place to set standards is the social service department itself, particularly in its dealings with clients. Some contexts, and possible standards, are:

Context	*Appropriate standards*
Clients' first impressions	Prompt replies
Answering enquiries	Named individuals as contact points
Phone/reception service	Clear statements of policies and
	Time-keeping for meetings and
	appointments

(Research shows that all these are important to consumer satisfaction.)

A mentality of service	Courtesy
	Providing clear information
	Revealing care plans, having open
	records
	Talking directly to children
	Keeping in touch with parents
	Responding quickly to criticism

Contd.

Context	*Appropriate standards*
Outputs of care	Identifying practice and procedures
	Care plans and reviews within time limits
	Child protection procedures
	Equal opportunities targets
The care environment	Reflecting the values of residential care e.g.
	private access to a telephone
	choice of meals and mealtimes
	individual contracts
	a range of leisure activities
	use of key workers

For each of these standards, indicators/measures can be set. For example:

Standard	*Appropriate indicators*
Service is prompt	Enquirers receive a reply within 3 working days
	Appointments are arranged within a working week
Face-to-face interviews	Interpreters are immediately available in languages specified as appropriate to the linguistic needs of the population
	Interpreters in other languages will be obtained within 48 hours
	Signers are available on request
Day Centre users are consulted about the programme of activities	Agendas for user meetings are publicised in advance
	Users comment on the programme through an evaluation form
	A summary of users' views is circulated with the agenda for the meeting

Raising standards

Standards should not be static, but evolve in the light of review and evaluation. The process of raising standards acts as a ratchet: standards are publicised and met over a period, but the expectations of consumers and professionals increase. There have been many examples of this in recent years — for instance:

— Provision of single rooms in residential care;
— Parents being allowed to enter hospital along with their children;
— Direct observation of social work students' practice.

Raising standards can be painful. A unit or department gains a reputation for good practice and staff feel secure: until suddenly the standards they have established start being questioned — they are no longer good enough. A department may make great efforts to meet policy objectives in equal opportunities and child care: but suddenly user's groups or black professionals start to question their practice with black families. This can leave the team feeling demoralised, but it also provides an opportunity for review. Of course not everything clients and user groups might like is going to happen: taxpayers have their point of view, and local authorities have to hold the balance. But by no means all improvements involve higher cost — important gains have come from doing what has always been done in a more sensitive and enlightened way.

BS 5750 — impact on Quality and Practice

BS 5750 of the British Standards Institute sets out international quality standards (ISO 9000) for an organisation; it was originally designed for manufacturing industry, and has been adapted for social care agencies. It does not prescribe specific standards for the end product, but asks for a detailed quality system. An agency wishing to register for BS 5750 has to produce a detailed quality manual, and submit this for external assessment. The manual should include:

— a clear policy for quality objectives
— staff roles and responsibilities
— staff training
— systems for monitoring and testing
— organisational procedures
— arrangements for quality control and internal audit
— systems for management information.

It is important to say in your manual what you are going to do about any problems that may come up, so that the quality system is shown to be dynamic rather than static. An agency which has already developed a set of quality standards and relevant indicators will be in a good position to register for BS 5750, the whole process can be linked with the preparation and assessment of staff for NVQs (as discussed in chapter 8), and the two together should help to raise standards.

At present there is a debate about how much BS 5750 will be used in social care agencies and how relevant it is. For a voluntary provider in search of new contracts it may be an important selling point, and give an edge on its competitors, but the costs for registration have to be taken into account, both in terms of registration fees and staff time. For a small voluntary organisation they may be prohibitive. One small organisation which decided to apply for registration estimated that it would take twelve hours a week of staff time for six months. From the point of view of a commissioning agency, registration for BS 5750 shows that a provider takes quality issues very seriously, but it cannot, in itself, be any substitute for monitoring or inspection. The purchaser has to be satisfied with the end product of care as well as the systems of quality assurance.

Monitoring standards

There are three main sorts of monitoring:

- Monitoring by the manager of standards within her own team;
- Monitoring by an in-house inspection unit;
- Monitoring/inspection of a supplier by the social services department.

In each case monitoring has two aims — to see that standards are met, and to help the person being monitored to raise them (these aims are usually called 'regulation' and 'development'). However the balance between them differs: if standards fall, the job of a manager is to improve them, while customers can simply take their business elsewhere. There is thus a considerable difference in the spirit in which inspection is carried out: a manager has to trust her team and let them see it — though not be so trustful that she doesn't notice what's going on. By contrast, an outside inspector can be more coldly critical — if standards aren't met, it is the supplier's problem to put them right. However customers will get better service in practice if they act at least partly like managers — understand the supplier's problems, encourage improvement, and give advice: provided that the relationship doesn't get so cosy that poor quality service becomes acceptable. Internal inspectors are in an intermediate position — they will report back to management (at some level in the hierarchy) and it is up to management to secure improvement.

Monitoring within the team

The main way in which the manager monitors results is through supervision, discussed in the next chapter. Supervision has traditionally relied on written and verbal accounts from the worker. If records such as case review and assessment forms are standardised, results can be put together to form local statistics, which can be used both to assess local need and to monitor the results of the team as a whole. Quality assurance can provide another source of control data

— for example records of when standards are not met. The trouble with this is that if quality records are seen by staff members as a way of spying on them, they won't maintain them accurately, so that the whole process becomes a waste of time. Therefore, reports can only be used in the aggregate, to show where the team as a whole could do better. There is no substitute for gathering regular, systematic information from users, either through questionnaires or users' committees (discussed in the next section).

As we have seen, setting standards is best done as a team effort, and the team can also help to monitor, through various forms of peer group review, ranging from discussion of cases to 'group supervision' (chapter 6). This kind of monitoring can lead on to problem solving by the group. One form of this that is well established in industry is 'Quality Circles'. These consist of groups of peers who meet regularly to consider difficulties in maintaining quality standards, and how to overcome them. The quality circle identifies problems in service delivery, and chooses one which they can control. It then considers what is causing the problem, and how things might be improved. To move from problems to solutions, the group needs a shift in gear to more creative thinking. One good way to accomplish this is by 'brainstorming'. Group members are asked to give answers to open-ended questions, such as, 'as a complete outsider, how would you solve this?' or, 'ideally, what would you do about it?' All the contributions are written up, without allowing any questioning or disagreement. The group then chooses a few suggestions to work on. At this stage they answer the question 'how could this be done?', and try to find ways of surmounting obstacles. It is important that the solutions proposed can be implemented by the group, and also that senior managers support the group's efforts and provide whatever information is needed.

Periodic review by in-house assessors (often called 'audit'). The Department of Health publication *Committed to Quality*,[1] based on information gathered by the social services inspectorate, warns against relying too heavily on independent inspection units for quality assurance. The problems they identified were the unfortunate implications of the term 'inspection', and the risk of giving inspectors too much work. A far worse defect is that it lets managers out of doing an essential part of their job. If they don't know what's going on, except at second hand, and in arrears, how can they act promptly and effectively to put things right? Outside inspection is more a way of checking on the manager than on her staff. A form of inspection found by the report to work well (for example in Humberside, Norfolk, Birmingham and Westminster) was to involve experienced practitioners in the evaluation of services, by setting up small evaluation teams, drawn from across the Department on short-term secondment. This has the advantages of giving practitioners some experience of managerial work, increasing the team's credibility, and improving communication across the Department. It works well if (as in Westminster and Humberside) the team includes representatives from several different levels, giving a diagonal slice of the cake. It is important that feedback should be given immediately to staff and their first-line manager, and that action points should be agreed. A general report should be made to the Directorate and Social Services Committee.

Managers should never lose sight of the fact that the main aim of monitoring standards is to improve them, and that the main vehicle for improvement is staff development. The link between quality assurance and staff development is the appraisal system (discussed on page 110 in chapter 6).

Assessing users' satisfaction

Studies of users in social work have shown that up to 80 per cent of recipients describe themselves as generally satisfied. Levels of satisfaction vary — older people, women, and people in higher income brackets tend to express greater satisfaction. However the notion of 'the satisfied customer' is not as simple as it seems — users may be reluctant to criticise staff whom they see as doing their best, and more dependent customers such as elderly residents may be afraid of the effects of criticism. Even an independent researcher will be associated with the service provider, and seen as in a position of authority. Sometimes clients may be satisfied with extremely low levels of service, which the providers themselves would prefer to improve.[2] One must also distinguish between the quality of care experienced — i.e. the way the service is delivered — and the actual results: users value good personal relationships with staff, but these don't always relate to a satisfactory outcome. Again, different members of a family, or different sorts of people may have different views about the service they receive — parents may differ from children, women from men, and carers from the people being looked after.

It follows that simple questionnaires, or rating scales on global satisfaction will not yield reliable results, and cannot be the only measure of the quality of service. Tests of user satisfaction should include some in-depth interviews or group discussions in order to get below the surface. From these it may be possible to construct lists of questions which deal with the *details* of a user's experience in a factual way, so that the answers are less likely to be fudged. If surveys are to be used on a large scale (say with more than 60 respondents), the soundest approach is to use Repertory Grid — a technique that ensures that questions are asked in a form that makes sense to respondents. The technique doesn't need an expert to run it and can be learnt from a short course or a book.[3] Studies like these deal with the past, but it is just as important to help users to influence services as they happen, particularly in the minor choices of daily living, such as meal times, choice of food or television programmes, level of heating, smoking policy etc. Not all users are in a position to explain their preferences — indeed as Kieran Walsh points out,[4] in work with people with severe learning difficulties or elderly mentally infirm people, neither the user nor the provider may be able to evaluate quality. It is usual to rely on the views of relatives or carers, but sometimes there are no relatives, and the views of the carer may differ from the wishes of the user. One solution is to introduce an independent visitor, or an advocate from an outside organisation, to supplement the views of in-house management.

Users' forums and self-advocacy groups

In day centres or residential care homes, centre committees or members councils are often found. These are seen by staff as a way of monitoring services, but research shows that users with learning difficulties may be less certain.[5] Committee members found it hard to raise anything other than safe issues, and felt that even when they were consulted, it was still the boss who decided: in any case there was only so much that the manager could do, because of lack of resources. Some key questions are:

— How the user's committee links with staff
— How suggestions are followed up, and who reports back on progress
— Whether there is a channel of communication direct to the management committee
— Whether members are clear about what can be influenced within the home and what is dependent on outside decisions
— Whether users are involved in interviewing new staff, and have a role in training.

Sometimes a users committee may be linked to an independent self-advocacy organisation such as People First, or Advocacy in Action.

The role of self-advocacy groups includes:

— Representing and helping people (usually those with learning difficulties or disabilities)
— Encouraging members to speak out

— Improving the public image, and countering stigma or stereotypes
— Increasing awareness among professionals
— Working to improve services
— Building up social networks and developing members' confidence.

Because they are independent, self-advocacy groups can be influential: they are the main source of advocates in individual cases, and may also serve on working parties and contribute to policy documents.

Users' forums draw together different user groups. they may be on-going, or convened for a particular purpose, such as consultation on the community care plan. The problem is to decide how representative the groups really are — it may be necessary to do a trawl in order to see if there are any others, particularly ethnic minority groups. Holding a forum needs careful planning, dealing with matters such as accessibility for wheelchairs, facilities for signing or audio-loop, interpreters, and material available in translation. It is also crucial that Social Services managers really want to hear what is said, and are not just going through the motions.

5.6   Inspection

The Registered Homes Act 1984 introduced registration and inspection of private and voluntary residential care homes by the local authority, and of nursing homes by the health authority. The NHS and Community Care Act extended this to local authority maintained homes. The Children Act established registration and inspection of independent children's homes and boarding schools, and inspection of maintained community homes. Since 1991, local authorities have had to establish an arms-length inspection unit, to set up an advisory committee, and prepare an annual report. The inspection unit is usually responsible to the Director of Social Services, but a 1992 consultative paper suggested it should be transferred to the Chief Executive's department.

The purpose of inspection is to provide quality control information, independent of line management and the structures of commissioning and contracting. The unit is at arms length from providers, and must be seen to be even-handed between in-house suppliers and independent suppliers. As units have developed it has become clear that there are a number of problems with this role:

— Private suppliers are suspicious that the inspector may not demand the same standards from local authority homes.

— Managers of in-house units feel that the inspector makes unreasonable demands, and ought to understand their problems better.[6]

— Private and voluntary organisations with homes in different localities complain of differing standards and ask for national ones.

— The staffing of inspection units varies in quality, and is sometimes insufficient for the workload.

— There is still an overlap between client groups served by registered homes and nursing homes, but there is often little contact between local authority and health authority inspectors (except in the case of dual registration). Joint working in inspection units has begun in a few authorities (such as Newcastle).

— There is some doubt about how the findings of the inspection report are fed back into decisions about commissioning and contracting.

So what does inspection involve, and what should a provider expect from the registration and inspection officer? Inspection, like monitoring generally, combines the two functions of regulation and development.

(a) **Regulation** is the primary objective; inspection is a safeguard for vulnerable clients who are often not in a position to complain and may not have family or friends to speak up for them. Minimum standards are set out in *Home Life*,[7] originally published in 1984, and likely soon to be revised; the Department of Health has published detailed guidance on standards for each client group in residential care, and in the light of these, each authority sets its own standards. The inspection visit aims to ensure that standards are met, and to set up and monitor any necessary programmes for improvement. Compliance can normally be secured by informal sanctions such as fear of losing business, or the prospect of bad publicity. If these don't work, maintained homes can merely be reported to the Committee, but private homes can suffer legal sanctions under the Registered Homes Act. It is harder to withdraw a registration than to refuse it in the first place, so it is important to be sure in advance that standards are acceptable. Committees don't always back the inspector, partly because of doubts about what will happen to residents if the home has to close.

(b) **Development.**   The best way to improve standards is through a partnership with managers and proprietors. A registered care home will have one substantial visit a year, plus one follow-up. Each visit will check the issues that caused concern last time, and review progress on implementing recommendations. An inspector may disclose the main focus of the visit in advance, and ask for answers to specific questions. Unannounced visits can be used to check on service delivery and to gain views from users. Over time, an inspector may develop a supportive relationship with a manager, but it will always be important to maintain enough distance to be critical, and to remember the distinction between monitoring standards and actively helping to solve management problems.

The object of the inspection visit is to gain as factual a view as possible of the quality of care provided, and an independent assessment of the quality of life of the residents. One approach is to use a checklist, which has the advantage of standardisation, but the disadvantage of being mechanistic. Research by Gibbs and Sinclair[8] found that using the same checklist, different inspectors came to different judgements about the quality of care in the same homes. Checklists can be supplemented by directly sampling food and testing appliances, and by observation and discussion with residents and staff. Few authorities will go as far as Norfolk who, as part of internal audit, asked pensioners to act as inspectors and experience homes as short-term residents.[9] The Department of Health lays emphasis on training in the skills of observation,[10] but effective observation depends on being unobtrusive: even on unannounced visits an inspector is scarcely likely to go unnoticed and her presence will influence the behaviour of staff and residents. The same problems apply to seeking users' views; the most vulnerable residents are precisely those who are least able to express their views to a visitor, and most likely to express compliance rather than criticism.

With these caveats in mind an inspection visit might use a variety of methods, with the following structure:[11]

— An announced annual visit, with a pre-planned agenda; all documents to be available in advance
— A pre-visit questionnaire to cover all policy and practical aspects
— A discussion of key aspects with the manager, and review of progress on previous reports
— Discussion with staff on the same agenda to gain their views
— Direct observation of staff/user interaction
— Participation in some activity
— Discussion with a group of users (if appropriate)
— Talking to individual users and relatives (some of this may be left for an unannounced follow-up visit)

— Immediate feedback at the end of the day, with an emphasis on good practice and indicating of any areas of concern.

The visit will be followed up within an agreed time-limit by a full report. The manager or proprietor will be given time to respond, and action points with timescales will be agreed. Everyone needs to be clear about what happens to the report and about the status of the recommendations. This is good practice in any case, but if there is any possibility of sanctions, it will be necessary to show that the owners have been given a chance to improve.

5.7 Complaints

Complaints procedures are now required by the Citizens' Charter for all services, and there are rights to representation and advocacy. How effective are they? A conference organised in 1992 by the National Consumer Council[12] showed that users' and advocacy groups were unhappy about the way they operated. Among the reservations were:

— Lack of information about complaints procedures
— A professional culture that relies on discretion and benevolence rather than entitlement to service
— Problems in defining a complaint and putting it in writing
— Lack of support or advocacy for complainants.

Many users find it difficult to complain — they feel vulnerable and don't know how professionals will react. They don't like to raise matters which may be seen as unimportant, especially if the worker is busy. They don't want to be seen as moaners, and feel that they ought to be grateful for the service. They may never have thought about the possibility of complaining, or they may be frightened of the consequences. In services such as home care, where users pay for the service, there may be less reluctance.

Because social work emphasises the value of relationships, social workers are apt to see a complaint about the service as a personal attack on themselves. A social worker whose work is complained about will need help to look at these issues. Sometimes the job of the manager will be to support staff who receive complaints, but in others the complaint may come directly to them, and they will have the task of passing it on.

All users should have access to information about complaints procedures. This may be in the form of a brochure, backed up by posters and other publicity. Some authorities use tear-off postcards, or one-stop shops in the High Street, so that users don't have to go directly to the service provider with their complaint.

The first stop for complaints is front-line workers, especially receptionists and care staff. These people need training, to help them imagine the feelings of someone with a complaint — often anger, powerlessness and fear, combined with a wish to put matters to rights. They can then look at their own possible reactions, such as dismissiveness, defensiveness, making light of the complaint, or taking it personally — or responding in the way set out below.

On receiving a complaint, the main steps are:

— Listen to the complainant; encourage them to say how they feel, and accept that they have a right to complain.

— Get as much detail as possible and write it down, checking back carefully.

— Suspend judgement and concentrate on getting a full and accurate story; avoid being pulled into expressions of opinion at an early stage.

— Don't try to explain the complaint away or minimise its importance — e.g. by suggesting that other people are far worse off.

— Avoid putting the responsibility on someone else, such as the committee, the council or the government.

— Explain the formal and informal stages of the complaints procedure; identify which stage the complaint is at, and who will be involved at the next stage; write all this down and give out a leaflet (checking that the complainant can read it).

— Explore the need for advocacy.

— Check carefully what the user wants to happen (ranking techniques can be useful here), and agree the next steps, noting what is decided.

Often there is a stage in the informal procedures when a complaint comes to the manager for mediation. This has its risks: the manager probably knows about the case already, and has her own views; she certainly has a view of the worker. She may be caught between a need to give the complainant a fair hearing, and a wish to support the worker and avoid jeopardising a working relationship. Alternatively she may be quite happy to have some points she has already made to the worker pushed home. In either case she should suspend judgement and concentrate on the complaint, leaving the working relationship for future attention. The manager must also find out whether the user wants to make the complaint formal, and should beware of trying to cool out trouble.

If the complaint is justified, the complainant has a right to redress. Often things can be sorted out fairly easily — meals can be served hotter, toilet paper can be provided, and the fridge cleaned out. Dissatisfactions with relationships are more difficult. In many cases the complainant is looking for an apology, plus an assurance that it won't happen again (users often remark that their reason for complaining is that they wouldn't like to see anyone else suffer in the same way). Professionals, however, find it difficult to apologise: they made arrangements which they believed were in the best interest of clients, and it comes as a shock to find that this belief isn't shared. Besides, even though social workers are paid, they often feel that they do their best, and that users should be grateful, or at least uncomplaining. It may help to consider some of these issues before complaints arise, so that professional presumptions of always knowing best can be examined in an uncharged atmosphere. The complainant may also want a change of worker, and this should be arranged. Some complaints will be about matters which are outside the control of the unit; in these cases it is important to say what representations will be made and to whom, and to arrange feedback.

Notes

1   Department of Health (1992) *Committed to Quality: Quality Assurance in Social Services Departments*.
2   Fisher, M. (1983) *Speaking of Clients* Community Care Monographs and Cheetham, J., Fuller, R., McIvor, G., Petch, A. (1992) *Evaluating Social Work Effectiveness* OUP.
3   Stewart, A. and Stewart, V. (1981) *Tomorrow's Managers Today*.
4   Kieran Walsh (1991) 'Quality and public services' *Public Administration* **69** Winter.
5   Simons, K. (1992) *Sticking Up For Yourself* Joseph Rowntree.
6   Norma Raynes (1993) *'An Inspector calls' Community Care* March 18.
7   Centre for Policy for Ageing (1984) *Home life*.
8   Gibbs, Sinclair (1992) 'Checklists: their possible contribution to inspection and quality assurance in elderly people's homes. In: Kelly, D., Warr, B. *Quality Counts* Social Care Association.
9   Cassam, E., Gupta, H. (1992) *Quality Assurance for Social Care Agencies* Longman.
10 See Department of Health (1992) *More Than Meets The Eye: observing quality in residential homes*. London: HMSO.
11 As suggested by Heather Wing in 'The role of inspection and evaluation in Social Care. In: Kelly, D., Warr, B. *Quality Counts* Social Care Association.
12 National Consumer Council (1992) *Getting heard and getting things changed* Conference Report.

6 Achieving results through people

It is one thing to set high standards, but quite another to maintain them. Inspection and checking are necessary, but nowhere near enough. What is essential is that the people involved should be committed to keeping standards high, and raising standards that fall — and this means not merely staff, but volunteers and the staff and management of contractors as well. Of course it will never be possible to succeed completely: all large organisations include some people who don't care, and a few who do active harm in a discreet sort of way. However organisations differ widely in their average level of commitment, and this itself depends largely on good management (though other factors, such as the nature of the work and job security, play a part).

6.1 Motivation

As we have seen, quality control depends heavily on positive motivation. How is this achieved? Motives are seldom pure, in the sense of unmixed: the greediest of us don't work *only* for money, the most selfless are not wholly indifferent to what we earn. A volunteer may turn out partly in order to get out of the house, but she is still likely to have a genuine interest in the work — or she would find something else to do. A good manager pays attention to both sorts of motives — doesn't minimise the more idealistic satisfactions of work, while making sure that the grosser needs are also met.

The theory of motivation is very complex, but it can be boiled down to seven main rules.[1]

Seven rules for motivation

People will be more committed to a task where:

1. There are no demotivators.
2. They understand the aims — or better still, they want the results for their own sake.
3. The rewards are satisfactory.
4. The work is socially approved.
5. The task is at the right level of difficulty.
6. People are allowed discretion in how they tackle it.
7. The task is enjoyable or 'satisfactory', in the sense of appealing to psychological needs.

The first six rules are fairly straightforward. Rule 1 — the absence of demotivators — merely reminds us that people will not be committed to a job if they have something more pressing on their minds, like trouble at home or poor health. There is only a limited amount a manager can do about such things (though she should be aware of them). However there may also be demotivators at work — poor pay or conditions, personal disputes or lingering grievances, and these the manager can and should do something about, since if she ignores them, the motivators discussed below may lose a lot of their effect.

The other rules deal with positive motivation. Rule 2 states that people will be committed to a task where they want the results (which is obvious enough). They may also be committed to a task that will benefit someone else, provided the aims are clear: tasks that seem aimless are a total turn-off. Rule 3, states that people will be committed where the rewards are satisfactory — 'rewards' meaning those that are external to the job (as opposed to inherent job satisfaction). For most people — other than volunteer helpers — the main reward is money. If pay is less than people regard as their due, motivation generally suffers (the reverse doesn't seem to be true — people paid over the odds don't try any harder). Rule 4 states that people will be encouraged if the job they do carries prestige, or is regarded as worthy by people whose opinion they value — including their own.

At this point, Rule 5 becomes significant: the task must be at the right level of difficulty. Aims can only act as a motivator if people believe that they are achievable: a task that seems impossible will fail to motivate, since despair or cynicism set in. Tasks motivate if they are hard enough to be stretching, but not so hard as to suggest certain defeat. People vary in the level of challenge they will accept, but for everyone there is an optimum level.

Rule 6 states that people will be motivated if they have a say in the decisions, and discretion in how they themselves operate. This derives from the earlier rules: if you are given a job to do where all the decisions have already been taken, most of the challenge will have been destroyed. So will any sense of pride or self-respect — no one wants to see themselves as a robot.

The rules so far apply to most people — albeit in different strengths. Some people may be more heavily motivated by money, others by a sense of public duty, but it is rare to find someone who is wholly motivated by one, and indifferent to the other. Rule 7 is rather different, being concerned with *individual* preferences. It is therefore worth pausing at this point, to see how the rules so far may apply to social work as a profession. Taking first the question of rewards, pay in social work (and profits for service providers) are not particularly high, but they are probably seen as reasonable within the context of the public sector. Someone who was strongly financially motivated would probably not have entered the profession in the first place. There can, however, be a demotivating effect for people who find themselves in early middle age with much higher expenses (through the need to bring up children, support relatives etc.). This would matter less if there weren't other demotivators at work. Social workers often enter the profession with a high sense of public duty, but they don't find that the public values them in the same way as it does (say) doctors and nurses (and they risk savage attacks in the press if anything goes wrong). The reasons for this are complex, but the effects can be damaging. Secondly, the aims of social work may seem clear and socially beneficial, but achievement of the task set often comes to seem impossible. There is no end to the demand upon impossibly stretched resources; human deficiencies, follies and vices do not respond readily to treatment; and society itself can come to seem the cause of monstrous problems that it makes no serious effort to cure. None of this *needs* to make people demotivated, but it is a climate of feeling that managers must contend with.

6.2   Motivation and psychological needs

The last rule — Rule 7 — deals with the different forms of enjoyment and satisfaction that different people get from work. Enjoyment can often be the strongest motivator of all, capable of replacing all the others. Enjoyment can come from solving work problems, or from the humour and comradeship of working with

other people. But there are other forms of satisfaction that one could
not really call enjoyment: for example, a sense of achievement, the
chance to exercise power, to find out something new, to improve
oneself, to carry out what one regards as a duty, or to stretch oneself
by enduring something difficult, dangerous or unpleasant. The
research that helps most to explain differences of motivation is that
concerned with 'psychological needs'.[2]

The starting point is to distinguish between needs and drives.
This begins at the physiological level, where a 'need' is something
you die for lack of — like food, water or air; a 'drive' is the conscious
craving, when the need isn't met. Needs and drives don't always
coincide: if you are starving, the need is always there but the craving
for food varies in strength. Some needs don't give rise to drives at all
— you can die of some forms of vitamin deficiency without being
driven to look for the kind of food that would save your life.

The concept has been extended to 'psychological needs'. If they
are not fulfilled, you don't actually die, but you will be unhappy and
subject to stress. The concept was originated in the 1930s by the
psychiatrist H.A. Murray, who from his clinical work proposed a
long list of needs. His work was taken up by the psychologist D.C.
McClelland, who concentrated on the needs that seemed to be of
greatest importance to motivation at work — the needs for achievement, friendship ('affiliation'), and power. His work has been very
fruitful: he established measures for these needs, which can make
useful predictions about how both individuals and societies will
behave. What is most significant is that needs vary widely between
one individual and another: people whose needs are far apart may
find each other's behaviour incomprehensible or repulsive. These
needs are considered below.

The need for *friendship* is straightfoward. People who have it
strongly will get deep satisfaction from working in their home teams,
their wider networks, and with their clients. It might be thought that
this was the dominant satisfaction in social work, and a dis-
tinguishing feature of a good social worker. However while it may
well be the mark of a good carer, in professional work a motive of
even greater importance may be the need for power. This suggestion
may be unwelcome — power is generally regarded as a disreputable
motive, and no one likes being accused of seeking it. However there
is evidence that the best-run and most achieving organisations are
not headed by people with a strong need for achievement, but by
those with a need for power: it is only people who enjoy it who can
be bothered with the constant process of persuading, encouraging
and chivvying that is needed if employees are to give of their best.
McClelland distinguishes between two faces of the power need —
power accompanied by high or by low self-control. High power need

plus low self-control is characteristic of alcoholics, criminals and entrepreneurs of the robber-baron type: people like this are sometimes magnetic leaders, but also self-indulgent and capricious. People with high power need plus high self-control are far more suited to manage, and likely to be found at the head of successful organisations. This make-up is also characteristic of teachers, in whom the power need comes out as helpfulness. It is interesting that a strong sense of justice is associated with this type of personality combined with a *low* need for friendship (people whose need for friendship is high are prone to favouritism). It can be seen that this kind of temperament could well be advantageous for social workers — to be heavily motivated and interested, while remaining controlled and detached. It is certainly true that social workers often have a degree of power *vis-à-vis* their clients that few other professions experience: those who enjoy it may bear up best under the stresses of the profession.[3]

The need for *achievement* is what drives people to get things done. They are not looking primarily for the prestige and reward of success, but the sense of getting there. This sort of motivation may be frustrated in an unending struggle like social work: it thrives in a context of projects that can be carried through with energy, and where success or failure is quickly apparent. What may be most relevant is the relation between need for achievement, and another persistent characteristic — fear of failure.[4] A characteristic of people with a strong need for achievement is that they set themselves targets that are stretching but possible — typically, ones that can be achieved about one time in three. People with a high fear of failure do the opposite — they set targets that are either absurdly low so that they can't miss them: or absurdly high, so that they have practically no chance of achieving them, and can't be blamed for failure. This characteristic can be found both in staff and clients, for whom it can be a considerable bar to self-help. Although the pattern is usually acquired in childhood, it can be alleviated by coaching (on the lines of Task-Centred Practice) or better still, by concentrated training (see chapter 8).

Fear of failure is connected with 'learnt helplessness', and also with a useful psychological concept known as 'locus of control'.[5] This is a test that measures how far people believe that their destiny is within their own control, and how far they see themselves as dominated by outside forces. People who see their world as within their own control are known as 'internals': people who see the control elsewhere — with fate, or the system, or just Them — are known as 'externals'. Not surprisingly it has been found that recent or prolonged experience of trouble or defeat tends to move people in the 'external' direction. More usefully, the converse is true — people who feel in control are more likely to try hard, and improve themselves. Even if there is little that they can do for themselves, the belief that they are a free agent gives them a better chance of using what scope they have. The implications of this apply very widely. If you expect people to be motivated, don't lead them to suppose that they are surrounded by immense problems, so that their own efforts are useless. Anti-racist training is of little use if it leaves white people immobilised by guilt, and black people by the overwhelming power of racism, and both feeling that there is nothing they can do about it. Again, empowerment cannot work as long as the people to be empowered have formed the view that struggle is hopeless: too much care (of the wrong sort) can be as destructive as too little.

6.3   Motivation and management

So how do these rules apply in practice? There are three main cases to consider:

1. Motivating staff
2. Motivating providers of services
3. Motivating volunteers (discussed in chapter 7).

(Motivating clients is of course a crucial aspect of social work, but it is part of practice rather than management.)

(a) Motivating staff

Some practical rules are outlined below.

1. Eliminate demotivators.   Staff are not going to work effectively if they have a continuing sense of grievance — through being underpaid or undervalued, because their working conditions are poor (nowhere to hold meetings, absence of books etc.), their list of cases is far too long to do the job properly, or because they object to aspects of policy or the way the group is run. This doesn't mean that all grievances can be put right — not everyone can be promoted, and not every desirable policy can be adopted. But a grievance loses some of its force if it is recognised and talked through, and the constraints explained — and if the team member believes in your honesty and goodwill, and that you are trying to be fair. In an autocratic environment, none of this is likely to happen: staff are not going to express their grievances if they think they may be punished for doing so; managers are not going to be trusted unless they put their cards on the table.

2. Be open with aims.   Always be prepared to discuss them. You have to demonstrate:

(a) That team members' personal aims are valued by you, and where possible, taken account of in decisions. If a team member is looking for a particular sort of experience, do your best to give it to them.

(b) That the aims of policy are clearly thought through, are stated honestly, and are not objectionable. A key instance of this is in establishing eligibility and priority for services: a social worker may not agree with the priorities that are set, but having consistent priorities will itself be a motivator.

(c) That where possible aims are explored democratically, and all staff have a chance to be heard in policy setting.

3. Delegate.   Allow team members as far as possible to run their own working lives. Delegate as far down the line as is practical — that is, where the subordinate has the knowledge and skill to take the decisions, and commitment to the objectives (it is up to you to see that knowledge, skill and commitment are developed). Where two or three people are involved, delegate decisions to the sub-group — provided they have the skills to agree among themselves.

However in delegating, make sure that:

• The task itself, its aims, and the limits to delegated authority, are clear and agreed;
• Specific targets are set: ideally proposed by the team member and accepted by you;
• The feedback you expect is defined — and that you actually get it. Feedback includes whether targets are met, periodical progress reports, and also the sort of contingencies you need to know about straight away.

One problem of delegating in social work is the high risk attached to some decisions: ways of dealing with this are discussed under 'Supervision' below.

4. Know your team — particularly their sources of satisfaction (what turns them on), the skills they value, and their long-term aims. Try and give them a chance to do what they enjoy, and use the skills they value.

5. Make staff feel valued.   If you take account of their aims, and allow them discretion, you have gone a long way towards doing this — the manager's personal manner is almost equally important. The manager must be generous with praise: if blame has to be given out, it should be measured, just, and given in privacy (while praise is best given in public). The manager must acquire the skill of thinking positively — spotting what is useful and constructive in what people say and do, rather than merely what is at fault. Sometimes we are inclined to blame behaviour, and shoot down suggestions, not because they are wrong, but simply because they are unexpected: we assume that whatever conflicts with our expectations must be at fault, and shoot it down instinctively. Above all, managers must listen: not just waiting impatiently to get their own word in, but really taking seriously what other people say.

Three examples of motivation

1. When a team was re-organised, one worker who had chosen mental health was allocated to the children and family team, and naturally felt hard done by.

The manager's response:

— Listen to the grievance; go through the process of allocation, and allow time for discussion; but don't collude in blaming the department — e.g. by saying 'I know it's appalling, but what can we do?'.
— Find out what aspects of the work in mental health particularly appealed. If, for example, it was the chance of multi-disciplinary work with doctors and CPNs, see if this can be replicated in the new setting.
— Find out what it is about child care that doesn't appeal — perhaps the need to take children into care compulsorily. Can this aspect be avoided at first in the new job, until training can be provided?
— Show the advantages of diverse experience for career prospects.
— Try to interest her in work with children by examining the overlap, and showing what skills are common to both.
— Publicly acknowledge the team member's expertise, and its importance in the new role.

2. A residential unit for adolescents is half full, and in the current round of cuts it has been decided that it will close and be reopened as a family centre. Some of the staff will be redeployed to the new centre, others within adolescent services. The manager will have concerns about her own career, but she also has a responsibility for the team.

The manager's response:
- Recognise the good work that has been done in the past
- Arrange some sort of rite of passage.
- Help staff see the advantages of the new way of providing for young people through fostering and community assessment.
- Point out the value of the new policy in providing another family centre in response to the Children Act.
- Find out from senior management what room there is for negotiation on who does what.
- Find out which team members have skills in working with young children.
- Make sure team members have access to counselling on redeployment, and union representation if necessary.

3. A manager of a supported house for people with learning difficulties inherited a system by which the manager arranged staff rotas. The rota was a constant source of staff resentment, while feedback from residents showed they were dissatisfied with the rigidity of this system, since key workers were not always available to accompany residents on important outings. The manager decided that designing a rota could be a team responsibility; the process should start with the needs of residents, then take account of the wishes of staff. Someone will still have to pull the results together, but the manager's role has shifted from directing to facilitating.

In the first two cases, the manager can do nothing much about the central grievance — that staff are being arbitrarily redeployed. Her response is: 1. to restore a sense of being valued; 2. to show that in each case the change is worthwhile, since it helps the central mission of the Department; and 3. to show that the essential aims of staff members are still being taken account of. In the third case, the manager can delegate — staff will be much more committed to a system they designed themselves (consultation can also help relations with clients).

(b) Motivation and suppliers

At first sight it may seem a tall order to motivate someone with whom you have only a customer relationship. However, powerful companies like Marks and Spencers take the on-going relationship with their suppliers very seriously, and provide training and help with their management problems. A social services department may be in the same position as a large company, being virtually the sole customer for a lot of its suppliers. It must use its power in a constructive rather than an oppressive way. Bear in mind though that there is one critical difference between suppliers and employees — services supplied cost money that comes out of the supplier's own pocket. Therefore suppliers — even idealistic ones, or voluntary organisations — have a fundamental aim of reducing costs, which may come in conflict with the aims of the purchaser.

Apart from this, suppliers have the same mix of motives as anyone else, and one can be imaginative in encouraging them to do a good job. One can for instance publish a newsletter and give publicity to suppliers whose work is of a high standard. One could have a prize for the Home of the Year, and invite the mayor to award it. Meetings and training days for suppliers can occasionally be organised — not everyone will want to come, but if they deal with real problems in a constructive way, they can be valuable and valued occasions.

You may or may not be able to affect the motivation of a supplier, but you may still need to ask yourself what their dominant motives are. Is the proprietor of an old people's care home merely concerned to maximise short-term profit by cutting down on facilities, or has she a genuine interest in providing service? The answer to this will make quite a lot of difference to the way you deal with her. On the whole, people respond to what is expected of them, and if you assume the best of people, they are more likely to behave accordingly — but keep a sharp eye open for anything that conflicts with such a rosy picture.

Building a team

Anyone who has ever been part of a strong team — for however short a period — will recognise it as one of the great experiences of their life. It is not a matter of good relationships or linked friendships — some individual members may in fact be quite cool towards each other. It is a sense that the whole group is aiming in the same direction, towards common objectives to which they are all deeply committed: a sense that all their abilities are stretched to the full, so that together there is nothing they cannot achieve. Sometimes teams of this sort are transient, the product of a training course or a particular short-term project: occasionally teams stay together for many years, and though the level of their effectiveness will vary, it will always be higher than that of groups who — however capable as individuals — cannot really work together. A strong team can be brought into being by a magnetic leader, but it can equally well happen where elements of leadership are shared among the members.

In building a strong team, there are five main elements:

(a) *Common agreement on aims.*   Obviously for a team to be effective, the aims of the work it does must be generally accepted. But common agreement means more than this: it means that every individual is committed to the aims, and sees it as his or her personal responsibility to make sure that they are achieved. There can be no hiding behind hierarchy, or blithely watching one's boss walking into difficulties: if she is going astray it is up to you to stop her — and equally, up to her to listen, and be prepared to be convinced. At times team members may disagree about the means to be used, but they will still try their hardest to make even the methods they see as mistaken, work.

(b) *Well-trained individuals, deployed in the light of their strengths.*   People differ widely in their abilities, but within a small group, every individual will have skills or abilities that her colleagues lack — a result that can easily be demonstrated in training. This is generally true even of trainees with learning difficulties, and it is invariably true of professionals: the person who is apparently least able will shine in the right role. The problem is to identify each person's strengths — harder than identifying their weaknesses, but far more important: weaknesses can and should be covered by other members of the team giving a hand, but strengths, if overlooked, may be lost to the team for ever. Some exercises for identifying strengths are suggested below. It can be a tremendous liberation to build up a new picture of what you can do, and find you are respected for doing it, and the sum of separate discoveries has a powerful effect on the team. However for people to display their strengths, they have to know their job — which is why professional training must also be sound.

(c) *A search for effective ways of working together.*   A team not only needs information about members' strengths: it must plan to deploy them, and to encourage its own effectiveness. The best basis for planning is a review of past experience, which will bring out further information. A format for reviewing is discussed below.

(d) *Conscious attention to matters of development, improvement and morale.*   In a good team, members are alert to each other's feelings, and the pressures individuals are under, and they will offer spontaneous help. However stresses and conflicts are still bound to occur: and when they do the team will set out to explore the causes and put matters right — once again ending with a plan that individuals take it upon themselves to operate.

(e) *Having the right mix of people.*   This should logically come first, but it is discussed last since it may be largely out of the control of junior managers (who have to accept the team they are given). Putting the right people together is an important function of management. A senior manager will say 'this team needs someone with ideas to ginger them up', or 'that branch needs someone steady, to keep their feet on the ground', and allocate or promote individuals accordingly. There is some excellent and clear-cut research on the make-up of a good team, which depends not so much on having talented individuals, as on the right mix of temperaments.[6]

Some exercises for team-building[7]

1. 'Process Review'. With an existing team, team-building starts with review, which should follow a period of intense — and preferably successful — activity. It is important that the main emphasis should be positive. Problems shouldn't be masked, but there is more to be learnt from success than failure, since from success you learn exactly what to do, while from failure you learn only what to avoid. Besides, reviewing success builds confidence within a team, while concentrating on failure, if it gets out of hand, can destroy it. It is important therefore not to let the exercise turn into an exploration of who was to blame — get discussion on to the future.

Head up three flip-charts with the following three columns:

Chart (i) What got the job done?
Contributions to success/causes of success/plans to repeat success
Chart (ii) What hindered the job?
Problems encountered/causes of problems/plans to overcome problems
Chart (iii) What helped co-operation?
Contributions to success/causes of success/plans to repeat success.

Take the three charts one at a time. Allow two minutes' silent note-taking, and then ask for answers, which should be charted, *without* any comments at this stage. If you get two or more answers, chart them all.

As a group, pick out answers that seem likely to be useful in the sense that they can be deliberately used or repeated and develop them further — remembering that a minimal plan has to specify *who* is going to do *what, when*. Allocate tasks — preferably to volunteers. Plan a follow-up meeting to review progress.

A formal review of this sort cannot be carried out very often, but it is useful to hold short reviews, following any significant piece of work. Reviews should always be charted, and any plans for the future kept safely, so people can be reminded of them. Successful plans can be accumulated to act as a standard of good working practice for the group. For example, the top management group of The National Society for the Prevention of Cruelty to Children evolved procedural checklists for topics such as running meetings, handling conflicts, and achieving consensus.[7] Some plans for running meetings are given in the next chapter.

2. Identifying strengths. This exercise should be carried out only after at least one successful review has been held. Even more than the review, it is crucial to keep this exercise positive, by making clear that you are exploring strengths, *not* weaknesses. Point out that most weaknesses are strengths in the right context: stubbornness can be seen as firmness, feebleness as readiness to accommodate other people. If, knowing your team, you see a risk that the session might dwell on negative criticism, don't hold it.

The stages of the exercise are:

(i) Following a period when reviews have taken place, get every member to jot down for each other member, 'What has she done to help the team do a good job?' Answers should be written on a separate sheet of paper for each individual. They should be precise and factual — *not* expressions of opinion. The more details are included, the better. Take as long as needed, but allow five minutes per team member.

(ii) Swap the sheets of paper, so that everyone gets what has been written about her. Each individual should then transcribe the comments about themselves — *without abbreviation* — on to a flip-chart, making sure they can be read at a distance. (This may seem a waste of time, but it only takes ten minutes or so, and makes the next stage easier.)

(iii) Each individual pins up her sheet, and people who made comments are asked to amplify them, so that everyone can agree how and where the helpful behaviour took place. This stage may need some strong steering to make sure it stays positive.

(iv) Give out the brief: 'In the light of what you now know about your strengths, make a personal plan to use them to improve the team's results. Let the team know what you propose to do, and any support you would like from them.' The manager should undertake to give individuals a chance to carry out their chosen activities, if at all practical. There may have to be some negotiation — for instance, if two people choose the same thing. People are likely to choose either projects, or continuous roles — e.g. improving the time-keeping of team meetings, or supporting a shyer team member.

When plans have been discussed, remind people that they are for real, and arrange to review progress in two or three weeks' time.

This exercise may be seen by team members as a considerable risk, and unless a degree of trust has already been built up, they may be reluctant to tackle it. However the strongest form of team-building is shared risk successfully overcome, and apart from its practical effects, the exercise itself can make a powerful bond.

Both these exercises can have a strong effect in destroying stereotypes. If people look coolly and positively at their colleagues' achievements, they will get a realistic picture of their abilities.

Multiracial teams

As part of equal opportunities policy, Social Services Departments try to appoint teams of social workers who more accurately reflect the ethnic mix of the populations they serve. Social workers will therefore often find themselves working in multiracial teams. In team-working, diversity is a strength, since it offers a range of experience to draw on, and the possibility of mutual learning and growth. However team members may also bring to their work harmful assumptions and stereotypes acquired in daily living. The most effective way to destroy these is by successful shared action, which makes it obvious how false they are, and where people work closely together, prejudices are unlikely to persist. However a lot of the job of social workers takes place in the field, and they may not have much opportunity for joint action (as opposed to occasional discussion and review, which are far less effective, since people may take up opposed positions). Moreover if assumptions don't change, they can undermine the working of the team, since people may be seen as representatives of their race, rather than as individuals with their own skills and personalities. An Asian worker may be over-loaded with cases from Asian communities or be asked to translate or interpret; a black worker may be cast as an expert on families from any Caribbean or African community. While being happy to turn to a black worker for help on issues of race, white workers may ignore her skill in other areas, because they don't expect it.

Where a black manager leads a predominantly white team, she may well feel exposed: white workers who are new to the situation may suspect that she won't be even-handed, or be anxious about her view of their work with black clients. Black workers may have high expectations, and be disappointed if they are not immediately fulfilled. The reactions of other professionals may range from mild surprise to consistently ignoring the manager and seeking to deal with her deputy. Within the Department, senior managers may expect her to spend her time serving on equal opportunities working parties, or negotiating with community groups, or advising the Director on what he should say to the press. Black managers now have access to networks of support and there are publications specifically written from a black perspective.[8]

It is still fairly common to find a team with a lone black or ethnic minority worker. Sometimes she will have been appointed on Section 11 funding, for development work with a particular community. The team manager should seek to reduce her isolation by looking for support networks or providing consultancy. It is also important to be clear about the development brief, and to make sure that the task is manageable and that progress is reviewed regularly. The worker should make a report to team meetings, so that she and her project are integrated into the team's thinking, and the value of the work is recognised.

In a team with a mix of workers with different racial identities, team-building should take account of this. The following exercises are useful:

1. Identifying skills within a team.   Ask participants to consider their own experience, and the skills derived from it. They should consider both work experience and life experience, and can be asked to head up a large sheet of paper in columns, or to draw two overlapping circles for personal and professional experience. Participants may wish to share their lists with one other person of their choice, in the first instance, and black workers should be given the opportunity to pair with another black worker if they so wish. The pairs can be asked to specifically consider the overlap between personal skills and work-based skills. Each pair is then asked to present their lists, concentrating on the differences between their experience, and the different strengths and skills that have resulted. Running the session will need some sensitivity, and people should be allowed to set limits to what they disclose.

2. Looking at co-working between black and white workers. There are many situations, such as residential homes and day-care centres, or in visits to black families, where it can be valuable for a black and white worker to be paired in a formal way, with their respective roles agreed in advance. This exercise serves as an introduction to co-working. Participants are divided into groups of black and white workers. Each group is asked to list on a flip chart what they expect of a co-worker of a different race, and what they think the co-worker would expect of them. Allow enough time for this part of the exercise, as the groups will have a lot to discuss. Some groups will need encouragement to draw on their experience and put down their feelings honestly. The lists are then compared, and participants are given time to challenge and explore them. Finally the whole group is asked to produce an agreed list of principles of good practice in co-working.

A second stage (carried out at a follow-up session) is to form pairs of black and white workers. Each pair is given the task of negotiating a co-working partnership for a specific job, in line with the agreed principles of good practice. While doing so, it is observed by another pair, who then report back on how well the negotiation reflected the principles agreed. If possible each pair should have the opportunity both to negotiate and observe. As in all simulation or role play it is important to allow sufficient time at the end for debriefing.

These exercises may help to reduce uncertainty and build trust. However the development of a strong team depends on developing mutual respect in the work situation, rather than on a team away-day. There are no easy answers to questions of how to set up joint working between black and white workers, or how to provide choice for black clients without overloading black workers. What is essential is a team culture in which assumptions can be challenged and feelings of fear or disappointment open expressed — and then practical plans made for improvement.

Appraisal

The main aim of appraisal is to improve performance. Manager and subordinate should jointly review the subordinate's performance during the year, and make plans for improvement — for example by:

— Using strengths to better purpose, and giving greater scope;
— Overcoming weaknesses, through training, support from the manager or the team, or restructuring the job so that the subordinate is less exposed.

Some secondary aims may be career counselling, identifying people suitable for promotion, bringing out problems and grievances, or for salary review (discussed below). Appraisal is normally an official activity, carried out in set form: if not, there is nothing to stop the manager appraising her staff informally.

In a typical appraisal system, the stages are as follows.

1. Both manager and subordinate prepare by filling in a similar questionnaire, to act as an *aide-mémoire* for discussion. It should ask:

— What were the subordinate's main responsibilities, projects and targets during the year. How well were they met?
— What were the main successes, and the main difficulties encountered?

2. Manager and subordinate should meet, to compare notes on the subordinate's performance, teasing out any disagreements.

3. Manager and subordinate should agree future action designed to:
   — Get the job done more effectively
   — Remove difficulties
   — Develop the subordinate
   — Plan for the subordinate's job satisfaction and future career.

4. Manager should ask the subordinate to propose specific targets and performance measures for the next year.

5. The manager should complete a brief report for senior management, which should probably be confidential (since, formally or informally, confidential discussions will happen anyway).

In private industry, appraisal data is also used for salary purposes — a point that turns the appraisal interview into something other than a relaxed discussion about possible improvements. In general, performance-related pay is a very good idea when the job has one overriding aim, whose achievement can be judged fairly objectively (paying salesmen commission is a good example). However where results can only be judged subjectively by the manager, the value of performance pay as a motivator is sharply reduced. In any case, it is only likely to affect the best and worst performers — average people in the middle will still get average pay. The best way to reward outstanding staff is to promote them (it is useful to have a 'senior practitioner' grade for high-performing people who for any reason aren't going to be managers, or not yet). The treatment of poor performers is discussed below.

Women as managers

Within the workforce of Social Services, women far outnumber men; in 1987–87 per cent of the total workforce of social services was female. Women are concentrated in the lower levels especially in part-time work in residential and day care, and within fieldwork as the majority of main grade workers, and a growing proportion of team leaders. Yet in 1992 still only 21 per cent of senior managers in Social Services departments in England and Wales were women. This imbalance is not explained by the age structure of the work-force, women come into social work at all ages, and often stay for long periods. Women managers are more likely to be found in operational or training roles than in strategic policy-making, and are concentrated in services such as residential and day care, or administration. The reasons for this have been well documented in publications such as *Promoting Women* (Department of Health 1992), and as a recent Institute of Directors' study shows, they are not unique to social work.[9] As perceived by women staff in social services, the problems are:

— The culture of senior management in Social Services Departments has a masculine style which they find unattractive
— The organisation of the work-load at senior levels does not allow for the more balanced lifestyle which they value
— The path to promotion does not allow for career breaks or flexible patterns of working
— Interview panels take a male view of what constitutes management potential
— Women are not encouraged to apply for senior jobs, or offered career counselling on possible avenues for progression
— High-profile activities, such as chairing steering groups, tend to be offered to men
— Women do not have access to male networks that offer information and support outside the formal organisation.

These perceptions certainly show the reasons that discourage women from pursuing promotion, and they need to be tackled vigorously by programmes of career counselling. At the same time, an organisational response should ensure that recruitment and interview procedures minimise bias, and that steering groups and working parties have a balanced representation, and that flexible patterns of working take account of caring responsibilities. Black women suffer two further disadvantages: first, their capacities may be undervalued, and secondly, they often feel themselves isolated, without supportive networks of the sort their colleagues have acquired.

As things stand, a woman in a managerial role (team or project leader, care manager, or manager of a residential unit or domiciliary care team) is likely to be running a team of women, but reporting to a male manager or a male-dominated committee. People in this position need to make conscious plans, both to improve their own job satisfaction, and develop their staff. Some strategies are:

— Be clear about your own support networks. Identify who in the organisation you can count on for support. Identify women (or black women) at your own level or higher, to whom you can turn to discuss work issues.
— Look outside the organisation for groups of women managers, and negotiate time to attend these (as part of your work).

— If you are really isolated — for instance, as a black woman manager — consider applying for consultancy. You should present the request as a piece of normal working practice rather than as a response to problems which might be interpreted as a sign of your inadequacy.

— Offer your women staff career counselling (as part of their appraisal or supervision). Follow this up by pressing for appropriate training or development programmes (a good appraisal system should do this for everyone).

— Publicise your team's achievements, and do what you can to promote its image, both within the organisation and outside.

— If your management style differs from that of your male superiors, explain the rationale behind it and demonstrate the results. As long as your methods work, you can be quite straightforward, without trying to hide them, or compromise.

— If you encounter sexism from your staff or superiors, use the equal opportunities policy — backed up as necessary by grievance or disciplinary procedures.

— When you attend meetings which are dominated by men, note the tactics that are being used, and practise your assertiveness skills: for example, by making certain that you are given a chance to speak, that you say as much as other people, that you are properly addressed, and that you are considered for working groups. If you have problems with any of this, have a word with the chair rather than quietly fuming.

Given the low representation of women (and almost total absence of black women) in senior management, there is some fear that the present re-organisation could depress their chances still further. This indeed happened after the Seebohm re-organisation in 1971. At the time most Children's Officers were women, but only a very few of them were appointed to the new post of director of Social Services. This was at least partly because heading a children's Department was seen as an extension of a woman's caring role, while taking charge of a Social Services Department, with a larger staff and budget, was a managerial task. The present re-organisation is emphasising a range of management tasks, such as budget control, contracting, marketing and community care planning — all of which lie outside most women's experience.

A study by Ruth Eley[10] suggests that there are differences in the importance attached by men and women to various components of the management task. Men ranked first ensuring that statutory responsibilities are carried out, followed by giving practical advice, and monitoring standards of practice: women ranked first the provision of support in the stresses of the job, followed by statutory responsibilities, and helping staff to set priorities and manage a caseload. Respondents to the Department of Health study saw women as having a more participative management style, with emphasis on supporting staff and getting them committed to high standards of service. The contribution of women to the human side of management is of great value, and needs to be recognised and reinforced. But if women are to reach full potential, they mustn't stop there: they must be encouraged — and push themselves — to acquire the new skills, recognising that staff participation is only one element in delivering a high quality service.

6.8 Supervision

In social work, 'Supervision' is used to mean the regular meeting (normally fortnightly) between manager and team member.[11] Its functions are:

(a) Task-setting and review. Allocating the work-load and agreeing aims; monitoring tasks; checking that policies and procedures are followed; and evaluating results.
(b) Support. Helping with the stresses of the job, and monitoring their effect on performance.
(c) Development. Helping staff to extend their professional skills, and find new ways of working.

In the main, these functions reinforce each other — both support and development help to ensure that a high quality service is delivered, and good supervision can have a powerful effect on motivation. However managers sometimes feel a sense of conflict between holding staff accountable, and nurturing their professional development.

The form supervision takes depends on the job being done. In case-work practice, a one-to-one session every fortnight is normal. In residential and day care and in community projects, workers can be supervised through immediate feedback on the spot, backed up by review and hand-over meetings. Where a social worker is seconded to a multi-disciplinary team, the function of supervision may be split between the 'home' manager, who may not have direct experience of the team's work, and a local manager who may be a health worker or doctor rather than social worker. In cases like this, individual supervision can be backed up by 'group supervision', in which cases or projects are reviewed by a group of peers, facilitated by a supervisor or consultant. The line manager will arrange periodic one-to-one interviews to co-ordinate work and review professional development. Managers of independent units will need to find ways to supervise their staff, but may not have any source of similar support themselves; they may wish to buy-in consultancy, or to seek supervision from some member of their management committee. Both supervisor and team member will have previous experience of supervision, and this can be built on. When someone joins a team, it can be useful for them and their new manager to complete a questionnaire which asks:

- What supervision methods have you found useful in the past? What methods have you found unhelpful?
- Are differences of age, sex or race likely to affect the parties' attitudes or assumptions?
- Note down your   Preferred style of working
                    Theoretical orientation
                    Value position

This can help both parties to agree on the aims of supervision, and clarify what is expected. Ground-rules can then be defined, dealing with frequency, subject matter, records and confidentiality. To make sure that the whole job is covered in a reasonable time and in a balanced way, each session should follow an agenda: this helps to avoid sessions being wholly taken up with discussing procedures, or getting bogged down in counselling the worker, without considering what is happening to clients. In order to avoid misunderstandings (and protect both worker and supervisor if a case should go wrong), a short note should be agreed of any action points.

(a) Task-setting and review

As chapter 2 showed, the cycle of doing a task (TaT) is essentially the same as that of personal development, the stages being:

- Aims (which may be constant through many cycles)
- Information
- Planning
- Action
- Review

In the supervision process, each task or assignment follows this pattern. A new assignment will begin with *aims* (or with *information*, if the assignment is a routine one). The manager will give whatever help with planning or preparation she thinks is needed, given the experience of the worker. For new or difficult tasks (such as attendance at court, a child protection investigation, a case discussion with a hostile psychiatrist, or challenging racist remarks in a group of young people), the manager can help the worker prepare and rehearse. The simplest approach is to ask '*what will you do if* . . .

the barrister challenges your evidence, the mother won't consent to the medical, the girl refuses to apologise? In the trickiest cases, role play can be used.

The *action* stage will take place outside the interview, though the superviser may sometimes have an opportunity for direct observation. In day and residential care, most work takes place in public. In child protection and inter-agency liaison, joint visits by social worker and team leader are quite common. Occasions like these give the manager a chance to observe the team member's work, and both to compare methods and style.

Review will take place at the subsequent session. (Where assignments are mostly long-term, review is the normal starting point.) All assignments will be discussed, information extracted and new plans made.

(b) Support

Review should deal not merely with events but with the feelings they produce. Social work is emotive, and if feelings aren't dealt with they may be denied or displaced, so that workers become distant from clients, or inappropriately angry or depressed. Reviewing feelings involves:

— Going over the experience to remember the detail;
— Recognising the feelings, naming them and owning them;
— Re-evaluating the experience.

Re-evaluation depends on recognition, and is greatly helped by describing the feelings to someone else. The supervisor is not the only person who can help with this process — colleagues and friends can be important too — but supervision should provide a formal opportunity for reflection. Sometimes the client's feelings, or the dynamics between worker and client, can be mirrored and reproduced by the supervision process.[12] Some common examples are reluctance to confront concerns about child care in black families, or failing to recognise that stress on a carer is leading to abuse of an elderly relative. The process ends with drawing conclusions for future action. The stages are:

1. Establishing what happened — both events and feelings;
2. Relating these to past experience, relevant theory, and practice examples;
3. Forming general rules for future guidance;
4. Applying these   (a) by the worker in managing cases, or
                     (b) in personal development, or
                     (c) in the future policy and practice of the unit.

This last may need discussion by the team as a whole. The manager may pull out of supervision interviews questions such as:

— *Do our assumptions about black families need to be checked in other situations? What practice literature might help?*
— *Does the policy of partnership in the family centre need to be reviewed?*
— *How can care managers become alert to signs of stress?*
— *Do day care staff have training in recognising signs of abuse?*

(c) Professional development

Part of the review process of each task should be to ask, 'Are there any conclusions (specific practices, or general rules) that could be applied to other cases?' The worker should jot these down, and they can be looked at again when the interview reaches the Development stage. Here the starting point will once again normally be review: '(We decided last time that you would be helped by more experience of X and Y — has that happened, and did you learn from it? Have any difficulties come to light, or unexpected successes been achieved, which we can plan to repeat?) Sometimes information may trigger off a new aim: 'Obviously you are very skilled at this kind of interview — can we arrange for you to run a session for the others? Or, 'This is giving you a lot of problems — let's see if training might help'. A fortnightly cycle is rather too short for having a serious look at professional development, which is a slow process, especially for experienced staff. It may be better to check each time for any new points, but hold a longer professional review, including a look at aims, quarterly or six-monthly (one major session being the annual appraisal).

6.9 Stress and work-load management

Compared with other professional groups, social workers show high levels of stress.[13] The first consequences are anxiety and depression, which can lead on to apathy about the job, a tendency to take time off work, becoming distant from clients, avoiding confrontation, and finally to physical illness or inability to work at all.

A good deal of stress is inherent in the job, which brings daily contact with clients in distress or suffering from violence or abuse, and with the debilitating effects of poverty and discrimination. There is also the need to take high-risk decisions, balancing the rights of clients against the likelihood of harm. Child-care workers suffer worst, since they have more involvement in their clients' lives, and less ability to maintain distance. Stress often comes from a feeling of helplessness — the disparity between perceived demands and the ability to cope with them. It is therefore the reverse side of high motivation, and satisfaction from task achievement. Trouble comes when work is so organised that satisfactory results aren't achievable. When social workers in Northern Ireland were asked to score sources of stress,[14] the factors mentioned most frequently were:

— Having too little time to perform duties to their satisfaction
— Rationing of scarce services and resources
— Meeting deadlines imposed by others.

(These were closely followed by client-related factors, such as emotional demands, and the imposition of controls which restrict autonomy.) It is clear that workers need mechanisms of support (few of those surveyed felt that supervision had been much help, nor had their agencies done much for them). Still more, they needed a work-load they could handle. This will never again happen in units that function through crisis management at the expense of planning. Again too much pressure will destroy any possibility of partnership with users. As Kathryn Ellis discovered from her research into involving users in needs-assessment, 'Only practitioners whose time was not strictly rationed felt they could afford to be human with the people they were assessing'.[15]

Managers have therefore a responsibility to see that their team is not overworked. This will involve:

— Clear criteria for accepting work and prioritising it
— A fair system of work allocation
— The use of a workload management scheme
— Work-load review through supervision
— Attention to differences in individual motivation
— Team discussion of tensions and disagreements.

Work-load management schemes have been advocated in social work since Goldberg's case review scheme was published in the late seventies.[16] More recent schemes have included weightings for group-work, project work and student supervision. The advantage of these is that allocation of work can be visible and public, and time can be allowed for undervalued activities such as liaising with voluntary groups. Examining the work-load can be an important element of team exercises dealing with aims and priorities, while setting quality standards can help a team to sort out the desirable from the essential. Take for example the disputed question of providing a duty service for callers. In recent years, many offices under pressure have arbitrarily closed their doors for periods during the week, much to the frustration of consumers. As part of a quality exercise, a team could survey the views of professionals and callers, and decide perhaps that the duty service should be open three days a week, but that other days would have emergency cover only. Provided this is well publicised, it may be much better than a five-day opening which is constantly breaking down.

Where there are criteria for eligibility for service, managers of assessment teams can be clear about the limits of what is available. Even if these limits are restrictive, it is better that they should be published in advance, rather than left to the discretion of a junior worker under pressure. Provider units will have their own service specifications, and the level of service will be determined by their budgets. Independent providers may be in a position to set a price which allows adequate staffing, though pressure on costs may push them too into overloading their staff.

Disputes and discipline

Nothing is more demotivating than a long-running dispute, or the slow grinding through of grievance or disciplinary procedures. The golden rule is to deal with them quickly, since delay compounds the harm. Participative management means encouraging team members to share in decisions or plan their own approach: it doesn't mean condoning slackness or indiscipline. If someone is regularly late on shift, it is a breach of duty as well as a requirement of good team working, and there is no point in letting the team enter into competitive bidding about whose commitments are heaviest, or the different time-frames of owls and larks. Derogatory remarks based on race or sex are flatly contrary to equal opportunities policy and should be jumped on at once, without wasting time on explanations and excuses. Failure to come to meetings flouts the team's working practices and unless it is taken up quickly the habit will spread.

Disputes may arise between team members, between worker and manager, or between a member of the home team and an outsider. Within any team, different ways of working will emerge, and as members join or leave, periods of adjustment will recur. It is important that disagreements should be discussed and resolved, without being allowed to fester: but none of this needs lead to real antagonism. Evidence drawn from therapeutic or T Groups has been used to suggest that rows (or 'storming') are an essential part of development. This fails to recognise that groups with an active purpose behave in quite a different way from groups whose sole function is self-exploration. At best, 'storming' is a sign that a necessary job is being done badly. Nor is it true that conflict enriches a team: once a row starts, any benefit from contrasting points of view will disappear, since people stop discussing in order to learn, and start arguing to win. Therefore a manager's most valuable role in solving disputes is not letting them happen: insisting that points are raised in a non-aggressive way, being alert to notice if any team member is behaving unreasonably, and insisting that different points of view should be judged on their merits — including views that conflict with the manager's.

The principles for dealing with disputes are much the same as those for dealing with complaints (chapter 5): listening, acknowledging feelings, carefully recording the facts, and making an even-handed response. If a manager is faced with a dispute between two team members, the first stage is to find out what's going on — in outline, if not in bickering detail. The next stage is to restate the dispute, shorn of rhetoric, in words that both sides can accept ('So what it comes down to is, Meera has always done Thursdays, and doesn't want to change, even though Thursday is the only day Sharon can do.'). If the dispute is self-contained and not too serious, the third stage should often be to get the parties themselves to sort out a compromise. Wherever possible, disputes should be resolved informally. However avoid the trap of treating something as a dispute between individuals, when a breach of discipline is involved.

Formal disciplinary procedure should be as a last resort. Attention to staff motivation, quality standards, good team working, and skilful management will all reduce the need for it. In one case, a health authority transferred all its supported houses for people with learning difficulties to the control of an independent organisation. The manager remarked that in the last year the houses were run by the Health Authority, there were 30 disciplinary hearings: in the first three years of independence, there was only one. Nevertheless where the offence is gross, or it persists in spite of informal warnings, disciplinary procedures will have to be used. In this case, a manager should get the support of her own superior, and stick strictly to the procedural rules.

Notes

1   For motivation generally, see Ajzen and Fishbein 1980.
2   For psychological needs, see McClelland and others 1953.
3   Another sort of people in whom the power need is likely to be strong is community leaders. These people may get on rather well with social workers since they share the same pattern of motives — which may not be nearly so strong in the community at large. Since two other characteristics that are associated with the power need are aggression, and desire for prestige (McClelland 1975) community leaders can be difficult people to deal with.
4   For fear of failure, see Atkinson and Birch, 1978.
5   For locus of control, see Lefcourt 1976.
6   For team building see Belbin, H. 1981.

7   For NSPCC, see Taylor 1992.
8   Such as Ahmad, B. (1992) *Dictionary of Black Managers in White Organisations* NISW.
9   Department of Health (1992) *Promoting Women*. See also Grimwood, C., Popplestone, R. (1993) *Women, Management and Care* Macmillan.
10   Ruth Eley 'Women in Management in Social Services Departments'. In: Hallett, C. (1989) and *Women and Social Services Departments* Harvester Wheatsheaf.
11   Supervision in social work has been extensively discussed and there are a number of useful books which explore supervision in different settings and give exercises for improving supervisor skill; see especially *Developing Supervision of Teams in Field and Residential Social Work* by Chris Payne and Tony Scott and *Staff Supervision in Child Protection Work* by Margaret Richards and others.
12   This is explored in a training video *Acceptable Risk*, available from *CCETSW*.
13   Bennett, P., Evans, R., Tattersall, A. (1993) 'Stress and coping in social workers: a preliminary investigation' *British Journal of Social Work* 23, 1, Feb.
14   Gibson, F., McGrath, A. Reid, N. 'Occupational stress in social work' *British Journal of Social Work* 19, 1, Feb. 1989.
15   Ellis, K. (1993) *Squaring the Circle* Joseph Rowntree.
16   Goldberg, E., Warburton, R. (1979) *Ends and Means in Social Work* George Allen & Unwin.

7 Networking and joint working

7.1 Formal and informal networks

A 'network' is a system of relationships which links significant people, places and activities. 'Significance' depends on the purpose: the network used to organise an outing for older people will not be the same as the one used to get a new job. Networks differ from social groups in that not all the people are connected with each other, and there is not necessarily any stability or continuity. The network is like a mobile, connected by wire but constantly changing.

A network is maintained by interactions; most people have core networks which are relatively close-knit and extended networks which are more fluid, based on occasional contact. Networks are normally based on kinship, friendship, or patterns of reciprocity: for example, neighbours who lend tools or take in post for each other, and work colleagues who lend coffee, share information, and listen to problems. All such systems of exchange have their limits: you can ask a neighbour to mind the cat once too often, and colleagues may switch off at the hundredth description of the horrors of working with the Jones family.

The networks considered here are of two sorts — client networks (discussed below), and professional networks (discussed in 7.4).

7.2 Client networks

In social work it can be valuable to identify the network of the client.

Constructing a network diagram can help the professional to see the situation from the client's point of view — and realise that social work intervention is often peripheral to people's lives. Note that the professional may have one aim and the client rather different ones: for this purpose, it is the client's perception rather than the professional's that is important.

Community care recognises that most care is provided by informal networks, but the elderly and those with disabilities are typically the people whose networks are most restricted — often consisting of a single woman carer, plus limited contacts with the social services. A network like this depends on bonds of obligation rather than mutual benefit. It is a key social work task to sustain and extend informal networks. Take the example of an African Carribean young man, living in care in a predominantly white hostel. Through discussion at a review meeting, he was introduced to a black independent visitor, who took him to a black church where he became part of a group meeting on a Sunday evening. He was encouraged to join a training scheme at a college in an area with a larger black community, and was provided with the necessary fares. Eventually he was able to find lodgings with a lecturer from the college.

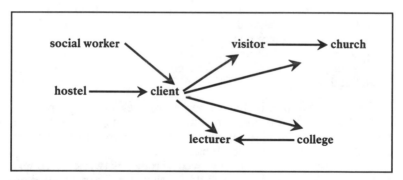

Figure 7.1

In this example (Fig. 7.1) the original professional links are supplemented by the growth of informal links, and the provision of practical support to enable new links to be made.

Not all networks are benign, and people may sometimes need help to restrict their contacts or find alternatives: young people may want to form new friendships to avoid being pulled towards drugs or petty crime. In the same way, the intervention by professionals into an existing network is not always constructive: the harm they can do includes:

— ignoring important links: for children in care, their extended family (grandparents, great aunts or former foster carers).
— insisting that contacts are broken or restricted, without good reason.
— building plans on the assumption that practical help will be provided, which for some reason never happens.
— introducing a social services resource that either distracts attention from existing resources, or provides a bad pattern to follow.
— in family conflicts, backing one side and rejecting the other.
— failing to recognise hostility or racist behaviour, within either professional or informal networks.
— expecting too much of key carers: for example, not realising that different ethnic groups have different ideas about what a carer's role involves.

Reviewing a package of care or a child care plan should mean keeping up all the links — with informal carers, voluntary groups and professional workers. One or two weak links can lead to the breakdown of the system. To give one example, the care of an elderly white Polish man was dependent on the following contacts:

— a neighbour in the flats, who kept an eye on his movements and popped in occasionally
— a day-centre place on three days a week
— a visit from a volunteer once a week
— transport to the Catholic Church and the provision of a meal on Sunday.

When the old man had a fall on Saturday evening, it happened that the neighbour was away and the Church transport had broken down. The provision of an alarm might have saved him from lying injured for 24 hours before reaching hospital.

Caring networks can be reviewed through network meetings, involving all the significant people, if they can be persuaded to come. The user is the key figure, and should be involved in setting the agenda, choosing the place, and inviting participants. The meeting will review how plans are working, and give a chance to explore how people feel. Take for example the case of a young Indian woman with disabilities, who plans to attend college. She lives in a council property, with free accommodation for a support worker, who is now leaving after being with her for two years. The other key people are two volunteers, the college counsellor, the care manager from social services, the organiser of a women's centre and the housing manager. The meeting might consider: the new support worker — the skills she needs, and how to recruit her; support offered by volunteers; and the college itself — ways of getting there, the timetable, and the demands of the course.

Principles of partnership

Although the word never appears in the Act itself, 'partnership' has come to be regarded as one of the cornerstones of the Children Act. *Principles and Practice in Regulations and Guidance*[1] sees 'the development of a working partnership with parents' as 'usually the most effective route to providing supplementary or substitute care for their children'. The Department of Health publication *Care Management and Assessment: Manager's guide*[2] puts emphasis on partnership: 'The new arrangements for care management and assessment are designed to create a more equal partnership between practitioners and users/carers with maximum participation by the latter.' However just to announce that a relationship is equal doesn't alter the realities: the professional has the power to take decisions and spend money, access to information, and the status of an expert; it is often the professional who presents a case on behalf of families to review meetings, case conferences, and other professionals.[3]

Take the example of a white mother and mixed-parentage child of 18 months being referred to Social Services by a local women's centre, because of reports that the child was being left on his own. As a result, after investigation and assessment, a case conference decides to place the child on the child protection register, and the mother agrees that he should be accommodated for a short period and placed with foster parents. How far is this agreement a real one? Does the outcome depend on partnership — or on the worker's specialist knowledge of early child development, her judgement of the mother's parenting skills, and the quasi-legal mandate derived from the child protection register? Has the close tie-up between professional opinions and case conference recommendations been explained to the mother? Has she been given a chance to present her own case, through discussions with the social worker and the conference chair? How far does the decision to offer foster care depend on the lack of other facilities, such as a place at a family centre, or more support for the play group at the women's centre? Impressionable people may 'agree' to things under professional persuasion in just the same way that they may 'confess' to things under police questioning — and neither the agreement nor the confession may be worth much. If application is made for a court order, the mother will be entitled to legal representation, but as long as the case is dealt with by 'agreement', the mother may be left with no support against authority. (In a case like this a social worker cannot be on both sides at once.)

Changes in practice can make explicit where the power lies, and try to limit its misuse, by establishing clear structures for consultation and open explanation of the reasons for decisions. Making these structures work is a management task which involves both careful supervision, and in-built checks on the way things are done at conferences and reviews.

As a result of their study on social work in partnership, Marsh and Fisher (1992) have suggested various principles that need to be followed if partnership is to mean much,[4] summarised below.

1. *Investigation is only justified when:*
   (i) *the user and carer explicitly consent; or*
   (ii) *it is essential for the fulfilment of statutory responsibilities.*

This rule is the most problematic. Social Service Departments are daily at the receiving end of worries and concerns from neighbours, friends, family, and other professionals. It is important to pick up signs of trouble early on, and simply telling people to take their worries away is likely to make matters worse. There is often intense pressure to do something, and there is always some fear of what the newspapers might say if a tragedy is not averted. There is evidence from child abuse enquiries that Social Services were not responsive enough to community concerns, and research into decisions in child care shows that early requests from families were often ignored.[5] It is therefore important to work with the referral network to sort out what cases should be taken up. At what point should the Health Visitor contact the Social Worker? When should the warden of a housing scheme pass on her worries about an elderly resident? It may be possible to gain the trust of a family in the early stages — preventative work can be highly effective, both in cost and in human terms. If statutory intervention is necessary, it should ideally be limited to the specific causes for concern — though this too may be difficult in practice.

2. *Any intervention must be based either on agreement with the client, or on clear statutory mandate.*   This distinction follows the intentions of the Children Act. As Marsh and Fisher point out, there is some confusion around the numerous cases where children are on the child protection register, since social workers often use the authority it gives them to take matters beyond the specific recommendations of the conference. Case planning needs to be supervised to make sure that specific goals and time limits are defined, that reviews are regular, and that there is a work-load management scheme. Standard procedures are now established for chairing case conferences, and work with parents and children should take place before the conference.

3. Intervention must be based on the views of all relevant family members and carers.   Social Workers tend to claim that they do this — a view not shared by clients. There is a need for training in the skills of intervention, such as:

— Design and use of written agreements
— To start with the problem that is most important to the client
— To consider solutions proposed by the client (as in task-centred practice)
— Skill in negotiation and mediation during family meetings
— Taking account of differing views
— Techniques of family therapy, such as circular questioning, which enable all family members to express a view.

4. Services must be based on negotiated agreement rather than assumptions or prejudices.   Some problems here are the worker's own prejudices, including assumptions about the values of other cultures, or the lifestyle of sexual minorities. These contribute to the ways in which power dynamics of race, gender, class, sexuality and disability are played out both in social services generally, and with this particular client. Common examples are the assumption that Asian elders don't need social work help because they are looked after by family members, or that Asian women express depression as bodily ailments, and therefore don't respond to counselling. Similarly a belief that working class men are difficult to work with can lead to the neglect of a father's role in a family, and a view that older people or disabled people have no sexual needs can lead to inappropriate plans for respite care. The worker must learn to open her mind to a range of explanations — including possibilities that conflict with her own strongly held views.[6] This constant self-questioning, combined with an ability to listen to the client's experience, without seeking to re-define it or to explain it away, is the basis of anti-discriminatory practice.

5. Users must have the widest possible choice.   Where choice has to be limited in any way (including choice of worker) the client should be told why.

Choice is limited by resources, but explanation at least is free. It does however require time and skills: also the readiness to let the client read the records, case notes and summaries. Quality standards can be established, relating to choice and availability of staff. For example, workers could undertake to keep clear half a day each week when they would be available to answer telephone calls. How difficult it is to let the client choose the worker depends on the organisation of the department. In area teams, where there is a division between assessment and long-term work, it may not be possible for the worker at the first point of contact to keep the case. However the duty worker could explain the system of allocation and give a list of team members, asking for preferences. All cases should be allocated within eight days, and if the client's choice of service or worker is not available, they should be told why. The duty worker should be present to hand over the case to the worker allocated.

A residential unit could produce a brochure giving photos of team members and statements of their skills and beliefs, to be distributed to area offices and other units. Young clients can be invited to visit the Unit for a meeting which all staff should attend (if possible they should also have a choice of Units). Selection policies should try to secure a mix of staff. Units might choose to move away from the key worker system to give young people a chance to get close to whichever staff member they chose.

7.4   Professional networks

The Acts put great emphasis on collaboration and inter-agency work. This can take many forms, ranging from a single transaction, to a loose network, to a mixed organisation.

Informal professional networks

As we have seen, a network is a system of exchange in which some of the points, but not all, have a relationship with each other. In any area, local agencies form a resource network, activated by workers who keep in touch, consult on the telephone, refer and seek advice. Keeping this network going and establishing links with voluntary agencies and community groups is an important task. Over time some of these links may develop into new projects for delivering services: one example is a health club for the over-55s in Earls Court described by Andrew Cooper.[7] Contacts between a social worker and health visitors at a local clinic led to them organising workshops to examine professional roles, and developing an interest in preventative health care for people in the early years of retirement. The club was established jointly by health visitors and social workers, and after evaluation, the district health authority included the need for more clubs like this in its plans. The initiative for projects like this often comes from the voluntary sector: a women's health centre used contacts with health visitors at a local clinic to initiate research on the health-care needs of African refugees, with a view to setting up a preventative health-care group. In both examples a lot of work was done to improve understanding between the professions, and dispel some common myths. Time was spent on looking at the different pressures of health visiting and social work, the differing priorities set by the legal and professional frameworks, and the details of work-practice. It was also found useful to unpick the differing meanings of commonly used words, such as 'prevention' and 'risk'.

Formal professional networks

Professionals also take part in formal networks, which come together regularly in the context of case conferences or review meetings (child protection is the obvious example). The aim is for the different agencies to pool information and expertise, so improving both assessment and care planning. Child protection inquiries have often highlighted gaps in information, and poor liaison, and government guidelines put great stress on the importance of working together.[8] A formal network will be set up in accordance with the guidelines and procedures of the local Area Child Protection Committee; it will have a structure, including a stated purpose, a designated member-ship, and procedures for minutes and agendas. What it lacks is formal authority over its members, so that it is dependent for effective working on its chair, and on conventions which ensure that everyone takes a full part. This push towards formal co-ordination in child protection rests on the hope that people will co-operate for the benefit of the child — ignoring the gloomier possibility that agencies may be more concerned with maximising their own status, resources and control over clients.[9] Professional rivalry and jockeying for position can interfere with decision making, and prevent cogent planning. The opposite risk is that professions may present the client with a united front, giving no scope for negotiation. One particular concern is the way in which assumptions about black families may influence inter-agency decisions and plans in child protection cases. To give one example, a seriously depressed African-Caribbean mother, whose 4-year-old child was originally placed on the register because of neglect, stayed out of touch with her family and had few black friends. In looking after her son, she had a great deal of support from a white neighbour. Over several years, although social workers, teachers and psychiatric clinics intervened, they failed to provide the mother with counselling or with training in parenting skills: nor did they encourage her to extend her contacts with other black parents, concentrating instead on the benefits of the child's contact with the neighbour. Following a further psychiatric crisis, a specialist worker for ethnic minorities was invited to the case conference. However in spite of her view that they should aim to keep the child with his mother, it seemed obvious to the other professionals that the neighbour would provide better care, and the child should be fostered. Instead of seeing the neighbour as a valuable part of a support network, they saw her as a superior substitute, discounting the value of keeping a black child in a black home.

7.5 Joint working

Joint planning between health and social services has a long history. In policy terms there has been a swing between periods of optimism when joint planning was the flavour of the month and extra money was on offer, and periods of gloom when everyone concluded that the obstacles were too great.[10] At present, joint working is in. By government decree, community care plans must be drawn up in consultation with health authorities and the independent and voluntary sectors; assessment criteria and procedures must be agreed with health authorities and GPs; arrangements for hospital discharge must be developed on a multi-disciplinary basis — all on pain of forfeiting government funding. How useful all this has been is an open question: the first SSI surveys of community care plans showed that the private sector had often been left out, and in some London boroughs, local representatives of black and ethnic minority organisations felt that not much notice had been taken of their views. A survey of the views of GPs in April 1993[11] showed that although Social Service Departments all believed that they had consulted GPs and agreed assessment procedures, over 50 per cent of GPs were unhappy with arrangements for referral, 43 per cent said that no assessment protocol had been agreed, and 21 per cent were unaware of the community care changes. In spite of the work that many authorities have put into publicity and training seminars, there is a lot more to be done.

Many community care projects are run on a multi-disciplinary basis. The 1983 demonstration projects were all multi-disciplinary, and in the run-up to implementation, a small team of the NHS management executive (Developing managers for community care) has funded a number of projects helping managers to develop the skills needed for inter-agency work. Most of these projects are in fields where there is an overlap between health care and social care services, so that joint working can replace demarcation disputes. In other fields, such as work with people with learning difficulties, or with HIV and AIDs, the division between health and social care is now seen as irrelevant, and what has emerged is an integrated approach to assessment and care planning, based on common values. This has led to new forms of training, which cross the health and social services divide. Ideas for new projects often come from the independent sector: managers of independent projects often know of pockets of unmet need, such as supported accommodation for people with challenging behaviour, and through membership of community care forums or joint planning groups, they can put proposals to health and social services, and apply for funds. Joint projects can be organised in various ways — as independent organisations, drawing funds and clients from the statutory services on a contract basis; as semi-independent projects, with funds and a management committee drawn from both authorities; as a partnership between health and social services, consisting of joint teams who retain separate accountability; or as a project under the auspices of one authority, with workers seconded from the other. Among the management issues that arise are:

— The need of managers for support;
— Accountability of staff (they may be supervised by a member of another profession, but still report to a line manager in their own organisation);
— The need to place the development of new skills before existing professional ambitions;
— The need for a flexible response, so that users are offered the full range of skills available within the group.

Joint planning, joint assessment and joint provision have their problems, but they are all easier than joint commissioning. In developing joint commissioning between health and social services, it helps to understand both organisational worlds, since there are key differences between them. At present, one difference is size, social services departments being larger and more complex, though as health authorities move to trust status, and social services are disaggregated, they will get more like each other. The problem of differing geographical boundaries is likely to get worse. Local authorities are under political control and officers have to argue with members and take account of political priorities, so that getting decisions often takes longer. The organisations have different priorities; for example in the field of learning difficulties, the health authority's priority has been re-locating patients from long-stay hospitals, while social services want to avoid risk for people living in the community. A move towards joint commissioning involves some loss of political control, and a fear of 'selling out' (made worse by the simultaneous move from running services in-house to contracting out). Both sides often lack the figures needed to draw up a budget, and there are differences in the way services are charged: for example the Health Service makes no charge for work done by district nurses, while social services such as bathing, home care and laundry are means-tested. There is always a danger that care plans will be distorted by what budget is available.

Multi-disciplinary teams

When people work regularly together for shared purposes, they become a team. This can happen within either networks or joint projects, and teams can be drawn from a variety of professional backgrounds. Their function may be *assessment* (as in assessment teams for learning difficulties, or hospital discharge teams) or *treatment* (as in child guidance work, psychiatric hospitals, or therapeutic communities). Multi-disciplinary teams have special problems, which are typical of the new world of shifting working groups (see chapter 9):

— The aims of the team and of the separate agencies may not coincide
— Team members who are still employed by their professional agencies may develop split loyalties
— Everyone may duck responsibility
— Democratic structures, such as rotating the chair, may lead to inaction
— It may be hard to keep a balance between being a specialist in one's own field, and joining in discussion of other people's. A lay person's common sense is not always welcome!
— Different professions have conventions about how one should act.

All of these points may increase personal or inter-professional stress. The solution is much the same as for other sorts of team:

1. A thorough exploration of aims. This can include the aims of the team itself, the aims of the separate agencies represented, the aims of the different professions, and the aims of individuals. The aims should be dealt with in that order, making formal use of a large-scale Why/How Network (which is ideal for the purpose).
2. A definition by the various agencies of the time and resources they are prepared to put in.
3. A definition by individuals of what they see as their professional contribution.
4. Establishing procedures for discussion and decision-making. The aims of these are that everyone has a chance to speak, that all contributions are given due weight, and that worthwhile proposals are guided towards action. Part of the agreement should be that discussion *will* cross professional boundaries, and that different professions will educate each other, without being either patronising or crushing.
5. A formal structure for routine business — minutes, chairing, and progress-chasing (the last can be crucial); also for sorting out

disputes (try to anticipate possible causes of conflict).

6. Agreement to review working periodically, and try to improve it.

An approach of this sort is a mechanism for securing the kind of behaviour that is really needed — mutual trust, open communications, flexible roles, and strong commitment, both by individuals and their agencies. It will also help people to understand the roles of other professions and their strengths and weaknesses (as we have seen, the best way to overcome prejudices and weaken stereotypes is by common action towards agreed goals).

7.6 Running meetings — chairing and personal behaviour

In all aspects of inter-agency work a great deal of staff time will be spent in meetings; it is therefore worth considering how meetings can be run in ways which are both efficient and cost effective. This section looks at behaviour in any kind of meeting, with most emphasis on the role of the chair.

Meetings differ in the job they are trying to do. They can be classified by stages of the Tackle a Task sequence:

1. Setting aims — including standards and performance indicators

2. Negotiation — where each side has its own aims, which have to be reconciled.

3. Information-exchange: e.g. within a team, an informal weekly updating of who is doing what.

4. Information + decision taking, e.g. case meetings, or local government committees (typically having a long agenda/many separate decisions.

5. Planning meetings (people leave with specific actions to take)

6. Planning + action meetings — people do the work there and then — e.g. producing a joint report.

7. Review meetings. How has the job gone? Future action to take? Plans for next time.

It is important to be clear on what sort of meeting you have to begin with, since the main job of the chair is to deliver the results that people expect. It can be disastrous if a meeting turns into a stimulating exchange of ideas, when what was needed was decisions and plans. It is also important to gauge the mood of the meeting: sometimes people are agreed on aims and want a quick resolution of outstanding points; at other times aims may be conflicting or blurred, or people may need time to make up their minds. The brisk approach that suits the first case can cause trouble in the second. Some guidelines for running meetings are as follows.

1. Prepare carefully, by going through each item on the agenda. Don't try to take decisions in advance, but consider:

— What *sort* of outcome is needed — e.g. exchange of information, agreements in principle, or plans for action.
— Who owns the item, and who else has strong feelings.
— Whether all the information needed for progress (and all the necessary people) will be there. If not, either get the information now, or postpone the item.
— The politics: points of conflict, hidden agendas, strong feelings, or professional rivalry.

2. At the start of the meeting, agree on what sort of result is wanted.

3. Set an outline timetable and propose it to the meeting. Don't try to keep to it rigidly, but if an item is far exceeding its allotted time, this may suggest that it should be dealt with some other way — remitted to an individual, or postponed to a special meeting.

4. As each main item comes up, check the aims (except where items are routine or recurrent, so that the aims are obvious).

5. Be democratic about the content of the meeting, but not necessarily about its *process*: e.g. be tough on red herrings (but check that they really are irrelevant). Make a (publicly visible) list of significant items raised out of order, so that they can be returned to later (this stops people jumping up every two minutes with the same point).

6. In dealing with aims or information, be open and democratic — make sure everyone contributes. In making plans (who does what, when) you may need to be more decisive. Don't try to plan as a committee, but invite volunteers for specific jobs.

7. Watch the meeting, and make sure everyone is getting their points across, and no one is being put down. Since it is difficult to observe if you are heavily involved yourself consider persuading someone else, who is less involved on particular items, to observe the meeting and identify any problems — constant over-talking, or one person dominating the discussion. In cases of serious difficulty, consider bringing in an outsider with a brief to watch and report back on the process — a sort of low-key facilitator's role. Whatever

arrangements you propose must obviously be cleared with the meeting.

8. For longish single items, use TaT as agenda (for aim-setting, use a Why/How network). Sum up, being aware of TaT stage reached.

9. Use a flip chart (either charting in person, or delegating): it should be written on in thick, felt-tip pen, and placed where everyone can see, since it will often be the focus of attention. Use it to record not only decisions, but points of information, suggestions and ideas, just as they occur, preferably in the speaker's words. The benefits are:

— The group all focus on the same point of discussion
— Ideas aren't lost
— People shut up once their point has been recorded, so that repetition and overtalking are reduced
— People can read through the discussion so far, and get a picture of the arguments
— There is a detailed, agreed, record, using participants' own words.

10. If a meeting is recurrent, from time to time hold a formal review of its process. Are people satisfied with the outcome, does everyone feel they get their points across, are there lingering misunderstandings, or emotional problems? At the same time, what are the meeting's achievements and successes, and how can they be built on for the future? End up with definite plans (who will do what, when) for improvement.

11. Things that go wrong:

— If the meeting gets bogged down — points get repetitive or no one can think straight — hold a coffee break, or get outside for ten minutes.
— If emotions flare up, suspend the agenda, hold an *ad hoc* review, and discuss why. Try to end up with a plan to put the problem right.
— If meetings drag on in a self-indulgent way, make them less comfortable (some meetings are best held standing up).
— If someone is not taking a full part, discuss it with them privately, and find out the reason (boredom, hurt feelings, shyness or whatever).

If someone is unassertive, be alert to when they wish to speak, and make sure they get a hearing. One useful approach is to give them the job of charting: this makes them the focus of attention, before they even have to speak, and puts them in a position of some power, since they can choose which contributions to highlight or ignore.

A meeting doesn't have to plough through all of its work with everyone present. At times the best approach may be to delegate — break into sub-groups to deal with separate items, or remit a problem to one individual to study and report back. If as sometimes happens, a meeting is held up by lack of a simple piece of information, someone should be sent out to get it (the test of a good team is that a volunteer has already gone!).

7.7   Working with volunteers and support workers

As well as co-operating with other professions, social workers are likely to find themselves working with support workers and volunteers. The community care demonstration projects and decentralised community social work teams both showed that paid support workers can do many of the tasks necessary for supporting vulnerable people in the community. Providing a care package may involve a mixed group of paid, volunteer and informal carers working together. Managers need to use their professional staff economically, in the light of the mix of skills available, so that the job of a social worker may turn out to be co-ordinating and facilitating the work of other people. In the case of one client with learning difficulties, the support worker's role has changed from providing round-the-clock care, to co-ordinating the activities of a home carer, a volunteer, an advocate, and a local church group.

Volunteers in social services have been used in three different ways. One way is as a supplementary resource to plug some of the gaps that social workers can't get around to. Usually they have been asked to work with the client groups that professionals find least appealing, such as elderly people. This sort of work is often unplanned and unsupported, without any opportunity for review and reflection. When voluntary workers are treated like this, their work can seem aimless as well as burdensome, since the commitment required is apparently unlimited. A second approach is to define the volunteer's contribution carefully, as part of the social work plan, and offer the same kind of support and review as a professional worker would get. This takes more time, but it can be far more productive.

The third way is to build on the skills and experience of people who are themselves service users, or have had similar experience to the people they are trying to help. This way of working falls within the tradition of community development, and can lead to novel ways of delivering services. Take for example the work done by elderly people in developing pensioners' groups, and by women who have themselves experienced domestic violence in offering counselling to others. One very successful project established a network of parents to give support to mothers immediately before and after the birth of a baby.

The recruitment, training and support of volunteers deserves as much attention as that of staff. Recruitment should obviously involve some screening, as well as a thorough discussion of what the work requires. Volunteering is a widespread activity (according to the 1981 census, 21 per cent of people over 16 had done organised voluntary work within the last 12 months), and the people most likely to volunteer are those in mid-life who already have family commitments.[12] Although volunteering is partly related to class, volunteers come from all classes, and the net should be cast widely to recruit people from all sections of the population. Volunteers have valuable experience in other walks of life, and the possibility of using this should always be explored.

Volunteers need to be managed in much the same way as other staff, and their hopes and fears need the same attention. One source of motivation — payment — is obviously missing, but otherwise all the same motives apply. In particular, volunteers need to be consulted about the work of the unit, to make their own decisions (within limits set by their experience), and to develop their skills. It won't always be possible to have the same discussion of aims and ambitions with a volunteer as one could with a staff member — the interest might be regarded as impertinence. One way of dealing with this is through an occasional training session: a group of people can be asked about their reactions to the work and their hopes and fears, when similar questions to individuals might be seen as a threat. A progressive training scheme can itself be a strong motivator (see chapter 8).

7.8 Public relations

Social workers do not enjoy the same public respect as other professions with whom the public come into contact. Doctors and nurses generally receive warm admiration; no one actually likes lawyers or accountants, but at least they respect them for their brains, but social workers are uniquely unfortunate. In child protection for example — a kind of work where you might expect great public sympathy — social workers are pilloried if they intervene, and still worse pilloried if they don't. Part of this damaging image may be inherent in the job — social workers appear at moments of disaster, and preside over some of the most dreaded rites of passage — for example, the move from an independent life to a residential home. There is however a good deal that can be done to improve the image, both on the national level and locally.

The main overall problem is that social work is secretive. Social workers are known to have awesome powers, particularly to take children away from parents, but few people know what the powers are, and how such matters are decided. Compare this with the criminal justice system — people who may never go near a court know from television and other sources a great deal about the powers of the police, the rights of defendants, and the machinery of justice, wigs and all. The need for confidentiality means that social work is done in private, and hearings are in camera. Again social workers, like other professions, are not above making a mystery of their expertise. Two main components of casework — sociology and psychoanalysis, are notorious for the obscurity of their language and concepts, and clients may feel that their behaviour is being interpreted and judged according to mysterious theories they have no hope of understanding (if they have an ethnic minority background, the mystery is that much deeper). Understanding is not helped by the profession's passion for euphemisms. When these are merely intended as politeness (like calling old people 'elderly') they may be harmless, but when the language of care conceals the reality of coercion (like 'secure unit' for locked cell), the public may well find it sinister. Perhaps connected with the language it uses is the impression the profession gives of being both humourless and defensive. In terms of public relations, social workers have great strengths — their intentions are admirable, the people they try to protect are the most vulnerable in society, the work is obviously stressful and occasionally dangerous. The subject of the work is often fascinating, combining it as it does the extremes of tragedy and comedy. It is something of an achievement to make it all seem so dull.

On the local level, there is a great deal social workers can do to improve the image of their project. Community work depends on good relations, and the local media are much the best way of spreading a message widely. Most local authorities try to centralise public relations and minimise contact with the press. This is fine if the public relations unit acts in a vigorous and open way, encouraging units to suggest stories that need to be put across, but if it sees its job as simply keeping the council out of trouble, a great deal will be lost. Small private and voluntary schemes have even more to gain from good publicity, and have no choice but to manage their own public relations. The advice below is for them, and for any other manager who has responsibility for publicity. All organisations should remember that though talking to the press can be dangerous, not talking can be far worse.

In dealing with journalists, there are seven main rules to remember:

1. Their product is news, and one central belief is that the public has a right to know. They may also know that their readership relishes bad news about social services, and so be happy to give it to them. On the other hand, most journalists would rather be fair, and local papers at least do not want to create local hostility.

2. If they are told something 'off the record', they won't report it. One can therefore explain a problem in confidence, and hope that deeper understanding will lead to more sympathetic reporting. Your remarks have to be labelled 'off the record' in advance — reporters won't accept the restriction if you try to impose it afterwards. (Another way of giving information in confidence is to say that it is 'unattributable' — in which case journalists can use the story, but not reveal the source. This may be useful if you are whistle-blowing on some in-house scandal, but should be used with caution!)

3. Get on personal terms with the local press and radio reporters. Try to help them to do their job — e.g. by knowing their deadlines, and being prepared be heard on an interview, or write a press release. If you do this, make it punchy and short, and put what you most want to say first — a journalist is quite likely to cut your release down to the length he has to fill and print it as it stands.

4. Give the press any positive news you have. Invite them to open days, tell them about successes, and any problems where public support could be helpful — e.g. information or responses you are trying to collect, or volunteers needed. If you have satisfied users, encourage them to talk (being careful to avoid pressure, or unprofessional manoeuvring). After all if you run a good service the public is entitled to know, and most people, users included, like to see themselves in the paper.

5. When faced with an episode that is going to be publicly damaging, decide what you are going to put across. You don't have to tell the whole story, but if awkward facts are bound to come out, it is better that you reveal them. Honesty is usually the best policy, and it is nearly always stupid to tell outright lies.

6. If false statements are made in the press, deny them immediately, give the true story, and ask for a correction to be published.

7. Watch what you say — especially remarks that can be used out of context, or jokes or sarcasm that can be printed as if they were serious.

Notes

1   Department of Health (1989) *Principles and Practice in Regulations and Guidance.*
2   Department of Health (1991) *Care Management and Assessment: manager's guide.*
3   Ryburn, M. (1991) 'The Children Act: power and empowerment'. *Adoption and Fostering* 15 p.10.
4   Marsh, P., Fisher, M. (1992) *Good Intentions: developing partnership in Social Services.*
5   Packman, J., Randall, J., Jacques, N. (1986) *Who Needs Care? Social Work Decisions in Child Care.*
6   Ahmad, B. (1990) *Black Perspectives in Social Work.*
7   Cooper, A. (1990) 'Neighbourhood and Network: a model for practice'. In: Darvill, G., Smale, G. *Partners in Empowerment: networks of innovation in social work.*
8   Department of Health (1991) *Working Together under the Children Act 1989.*
9   Hallett, C., Birchall, E. (1992) *Coordination and Child Protection.*
10   For the history of joint planning, see Challis, L. *et. al.* (1988) *Joint Approaches to Social Policy: rationality and practice.*
11   'Can the rift be healed?' *Community Care* April 1, 1993.
12   Matheson, J. (1990) *Voluntary Work: a study carried out as part of the 1988 General Household Survey.*

8 Training and development

8.1 Training, education and experience

There are three distinct approaches to training:

- The first is *educational*. It is typically carried out in colleges and universities. It is an extension of the process begun in schools, and it concentrates on knowledge, understanding, and thinking skills.
- The second approach is based on *experience*. It includes training related to NVQs, and a great deal of professional learning in social work.
- The third approach is what might be called *training proper*. Its roots are in industrial and management training, it is based on short courses carried out off the job, and it concentrates on job-related knowledge, and particularly skill.

All three kinds of training are needed, and too narrow concentration on any one of them can be harmful. In the past, training in Britain often tended to be strongly educational — theory was more important than practice, knowledge and understanding than skill. Today there has been a swing in the direction of experience: training is meant to be largely practical, and the assumption is that experience backed up by assessment will do nine-tenths of the job. This represents one of those swings of fashion to which governments seem particularly prone. Twenty years ago, when training first became a serious government preoccupation, experience-based training was regarded as not really training at all, and was derided under the name of 'Sit by Nelly' (. . . and she'll show you what to do, love). Training was required to be off the job, based on a thorough analysis of the knowledge and skills required. Nowadays assessment of on-the-job training is enshrined in NVQ paperwork, while there are only perfunctory references to training proper.

The pattern of this chapter is to look at why one should train, and ways of established training need. It goes on to look at the official systems of training and education within the profession, and the relation between educational and competence-based approaches. Finally it looks at the third approach — training proper, and at its unique contribution which is in danger of being neglected. The chapter goes on to look briefly at how a training approach could be used with clients, and then at the training needs of volunteers.

8.2   Training needs analysis

Training is an expensive process, and where employers (as opposed to the education system) are paying, it ought to be carried out in response to some need. The process of establishing this need is called 'training needs analysis'. It involves:

- Comparing the desired performance (of individuals, groups or the organisation as a whole) with actual performance
- Identifying deficiencies that can be repaired through training (rather than through other management intervention)
- Specifying the content of training needed — knowledge, understanding, creativity, skills, situations to be coped with etc.
- Drawing up a training plan, specifying who will be trained, what training they will get, timing of training, and costs.

Training needs will look very different depending on whether an organisation (or a profession) is in a stable state, or there is a need for big changes. In a stable state, the idea is to maintain performance levels as they are or improve them gradually, and training reflects this. Professional staff are (or should be) regularly appraised, and a good system should supply the necessary information about training needs, both for individuals and departments. The training needs of employees who aren't appraised should be reviewed every few years, since both jobs and levels of competence gradually change.

There are times however when jobs are about to change radically, so that new skills are needed, and appraisal, which looks at the past, is not a reliable guide. Change like this usually reflects a shift in policy, either locally or nationally, and extra funds are usually made available for training. A rather different case is where not so much jobs as standards are to be changed — people are to carry out much the same functions but more effectively, and training itself becomes the catalyst. This has been fairly common in industry when firms suddenly find themselves facing new competition, or a downturn in their business prospects, or managers feel that impetus is being lost. (It is discussed briefly on page 159 below.)

8.3 Individuals or groups

The aims of training can be either individual or collective. Some aims for individuals are:

- To equip a new entrant for her present or future job.
- To repair an individual's lack of experience, or weaknesses of performance.
- To give a boost to an experienced practitioner (outlook can become narrowed, or skills not used for some time can become rusty).
- To prepare someone for promotion or wider responsibilities.

Some collective aims are:

- To help staff think through the effects of changes in law, practice, etc., or to present new ideas to them. (The Children Act has involved a good deal of new thinking, including the requirement to see things from the child's point of view — recalling one's own childhood experiences.)
- To equip staff to deal with organisational changes (new ways of working, responsibilities etc).
- To upgrade the performance of a team, department or organisation (this is a form of 'organisation development' discussed below).

Just as aims can be collective or individual, so can the training that people get. There can be valuable advantages when numbers of staff undergo the same experience:

(i) If the first people to undergo the training find it useful and effective, it has a good chance of helping their colleagues;

(ii) Returned trainees can encourage each other to put the learning into practice, jointly develop ways of using it, and help sort out any problems.

(ii) People who have undergone the same experience share a common language and common approach. If A says 'this situ-

ation is a real "Dog" ' (or whatever concept the training introduces), B knows exactly what A means, and both of them will
think in terms of how "Dogs" should be tackled.

For these reasons, people in similar situations (like new entrants
to a department) should normally all undergo the same training.
This doesn't mean they should necessarily attend at the same time:
where training involves experimenting with one's own behaviour,
having close colleagues around can be inhibiting.
Individuals should be trained on their own:

(i) if they have unusual needs — for example, if the training is
intended to be remedial.
(ii) To try out forms of training that are new to the department;
(iii) To equip someone to be the team's 'expert' in some special
subject.

An individual may come back from training saying 'it was all old
hat, except for X and Y, which are really worth trying': she can then
explain X and Y, and share the benefits with everyone. However if
the whole experience was useful, don't expect anyone to pass on in
twenty minutes, the expertise they took days to acquire: send other
people to be trained properly. Occasionally a department sends
someone on a course in the vague hope that some improvement will
trickle through to her colleagues. This is usually a waste of money,
unless the person sent is the manager, who can enforce changes.

8.4   Professional training: the continuum

The social work training council (CCETSW) has developed a
continuum of training, extending over four different levels:

National Vocational Qualifications (NVQ)
Diploma in Social Work (Dip Sw)
Post-qualifying awards
Advanced awards

These awards are recognised nationally, and are achieved by
taking a series of modules or units, which are given credit at
different levels:

- NVQ   awards in care   levels 2, 3
         child care and education   2, 3
         criminal justice service   3, 4
    (Awards in Care are recognised by the Care Sector Consor-
    tium, which brings together social care and health.)

- Diploma in Social Work (Dip SW): at various levels, from higher education diploma, to BA, MA or post-graduate diploma.
- Post-qualifying awards are linked to higher education awards at level 3 (BA or BSc degree) or at MA or MSc level.
- Post-qualifying and advanced awards are linked to the Credit Accumulation and Transfer Scheme (CATS), which was established by the CNAA and is nationally recognised in higher education. It allows candidates to accumulate both professional and academic credits, gained from different institutions at different times (within limits), and so offers a very flexible form of training.

Various principles apply throughout the continuum:

1. Training is competency-based, and concentrates on outcomes rather than content.
2. Assessment of competence takes place in the field, either at work or in practice placement.
3. The employing agencies take the lead in the planning and assessment of training.
4. Colleges work with employers to offer training (this is mandatory at Dip SW and PQ level).
5. No one form of training is laid down. In order to improve access, a variety of routes to qualification are encouraged, and learners choose their own pathway.
6. There is provision for the assessment of a candidate's prior learning.
7. Multi-disciplinary training is encouraged.
8. Assessment is based on values of anti-racist and anti-discriminatory practice.
9. Standards are maintained by quality assurance methods, such as monitoring and external verification. CCETSW appoints external assessors.

8.5 National Vocational Qualifications

The main new development is the NVQs, which have been called a work-place revolution.[1] For staff they are a flexible system by which they can at once improve their performance and gain a national qualification. For managers, they have both advantages and drawbacks:

Advantages

1. They can help to keep and motivate staff, and improve their

performance. Because they are work-based, learning can be tailored to individual needs and 'competence' can be demonstrated on the job in hand.
2. They recognise the skills and experience of staff in residential and day care who have not previously had any access to training.
3. They cross the divide between health and social care, which makes them suitable in settings such as residential care for the elderly and mentally infirm, or supported housing for people with learning difficulties.
4. Assessing the competence of one or two staff members can lead to a thorough examination of work practices, and so to raising standards generally.
5. The programme is closely linked to quality assurance, since candidates are assessed on their competence to practise to nationally agreed occupational standards.
6. Contracting bodies can insist that independent suppliers include NVQ training programmes in their business plans.

Drawbacks

1. Cost: all training is expensive, but NVQ involves a sustained commitment of staff time over a long period. To this has to be added the time spent by managers in acting as mentors, enablers and assessors, and by senior managers attending assessment centre or consortia meetings (some agencies give this work to training specialists). There is a risk that only large employers will be able to find the funds, so that staff in small agencies get left out.
2. Because of the cost, only a few staff will be able to take part. There is a danger of rivalry, and raising expectations that can't be fulfilled.
3. To prepare for assessment of NVQs, the organisation has to put its own house in order; equal opportunities policies and health and safety procedures have to be properly documented, and whoever acts as 'enabler' must be clear on the rationale and policy of the agency. If it already has quality standards and performance criteria properly defined, these will make the process much more straightforward.

8.6   The role of the manager

The manager's role has always included planning the development of staff, through supervision and appraisal. But with NVQ, they will have to do much more — advise candidates about registration, help them to construct a learning programme that includes the elements of competence, and check that the unit is running to NVQ standards. To take the stages in turn:

1. Reviewing current practice.   The candidate has to be employed in a 'competent workplace', to show an understanding of policies and procedures, and be able to demonstrate the five 'principles of practice' of the Value Base Unit (anti-discriminatory practice, confidentiality, respect for individual rights and choice, acknowledgement of individual personal beliefs and identity, and effective communication.) Are these principles explicitly recognised in documents such as the service statement, charter of rights for users, and equal opportunities policy? Are they actually followed in individual service agreements and the daily running of the unit? It is worth checking these issues before embarking on NVQ — nothing is more embarrassing than having to answer a request for the equal opportunities policy with 'I'm sure we've got one but I can't think when I last saw it'.

2. Information.   Both staff and users will need information. If the department is committed to NVQs, a training officer will probably run introductory sessions; if not, the manager will have to. In any case she will have to keep informed, to answer questions and provide further information. Any users who will be involved in assessment must also be informed; they are usually pleased by the idea that caring is a skilled job needing training and assessment, but if they have any doubts, their privacy must be respected.

3. Access.   Given that access to NVQ will be limited by cost, it is important that it is seen to be fair and in accordance with equal opportunities. The manager should beware of making these decisions herself, without open discussion (and consulting the union if appropriate). There is a danger that the large numbers of unqualified black staff in social care jobs won't in practice get any training, unless they are actively encouraged.[2]

4. Recognising and accrediting existing skills and experience. The first job is for the candidate to identify her existing skills and experience; these can then be matched against the occupational standards, defined in the performance criteria for the units and elements of competence. It is a key principle of NVQ that credit should be given for prior learning — recognising for the first time the value of experience gained both in work and personal life. To apply for credit, the candidate puts together a portfolio of evidence of competence, which is then submitted for assessment in the same

way as competence in current work. Evidence can be of many kinds
— certificates of attendance on courses, reports or records prepared
at work, testimonials from employers, direct comments from users,
diaries or write-ups of activities, video tapes of interviews, or critical
incident studies. As the system is still fairly new, the assessment
centre can be asked to advise on the content and presentation of the
portfolio. Staff also need to build up portfolios of their current
activities with a view to submission in the future (this may become
part of the continuing professional development of most staff).[3]

5. *Preparing a Learning Programme.*   A learning programme is
meant to fill the gap between the candidate's present level of
competence (as established by the review of skills and experience)
and the desired level as defined by the performance criteria for the
various elements of the unit. This is similar to the process of
supervision and appraisal. The manager will normally help the
candidate to design her learning programme, which is not (it must be
stressed) a collection of courses but a set of opportunities for
learning, mostly work-based but including some off-the-job training. Suppose a candidate is working on improving 'communication',
and realises that although she is confident in her interactions with
individuals, she is apprehensive of talking in meetings. What
opportunities are there for her to practise and improve? They might
include observing a colleague talking at a meeting, and then
reviewing the key points with her; a dummy run of a presentation;
making a brief interjection in a meeting; trying a live presentation in
familiar surroundings. Practical skills such as preparing food or
bathing can be learnt from more experienced workers; knowledge of
welfare benefits or legislation can be learnt through training workshops or peer-group presentations.

6. *Acting as Coach.*   The NVQ programme is a process of guided
development, with help from a 'coach' in the work-place. Again this
task will often fall to the line manager, as it is an extension of the
usual process of supervision. The manager has to observe the
candidate's performance at work, which may need to be specially
arranged. Feedback has to be given in ways that are positive and
help learning, both by identifying strengths and by making suggestions for improvement. Constructive criticism is essential if the
candidate is to improve, but the manager has to be sensitive to her
preferred ways of learning, and allow for previous experience —
people who haven't deliberately set out to learn anything since
schooldays can be reduced to helplessness by criticism. By contrast
some people are very confident, and can be dismissive of suggestions
for change; coaching someone like this needs a more challenging
style and readiness to argue and justify opinions.

7. Assessment.   It is up to the candidate to collect the evidence for
assessment and present it. The portfolio can include evidence of
various kinds, but the best is direct observation of a natural situation
at work. The episode to be observed must demonstrate the chosen
competence without disrupting the normal routine of users. No one
is at ease when being observed and assessed, but planning can help
them. Some points to consider are:

— Explaining the process to the user(s), and getting her agree-
ment
— Making sure that confidentiality is respected
— Placing the observer away from direct eye contact with the
worker
— Procedure for taking notes
— Whether there are any circumstances in which the observer
will intervene
— Introductions
— Expected time limits
— Summing up, thanks and goodbyes.

Direct observation is followed by a discussion, to give the
candidate a chance to elaborate and show she understands the
principles and values.

An alternative to direct observation is simulation. The problem
here is that it is artificial, but it may be the best that can be done.
Whoever takes the part of the client should not be well known to the
candidate, and should be properly briefed.

Some managers may act as NVQ assessors, in which case they
will get some training. Of course in one sense they already assess
their staff, but this is aimed at professional development, and is
known as 'Formative Assessment'. Assessment for an award is called
'Summative', being intended to judge competence at a particular
point in time (though the candidate will be able to try again).
Summative assessment needs a different approach, concentrating on
standards ('does this performance meet the criteria?') rather than
helping the staff member to improve. The more the assessor has
been involved in the candidate's development, the harder it is to
switch to the objectivity necessary for judging. It can be very hard to
assess a member of one's own team as 'not yet competent'. This
problem is compounded by the subjectivity inherent in assessing
interpersonal skills. No assessment is objective, but one can try to
improve reliability by cutting down on wide variations between the
judgements of different assessors. Reliability is improved by having
checks and second opinions, provided in the NVQ scheme by
internal and external verifiers.

8.7   Qualifying and post-qualifying training

The Diploma in Social Work depends on assessment in practice placement rather than in the current work-place. It may be based on college or on employment, in which case the student's line manager cannot act as the practice teacher. Managers will be involved in preparing staff to act as practice teachers, and in ensuring that there are suitable learning opportunities for students placed in the agency.

One form of post-qualifying award that is becoming more common is to become a practice teacher. The process of submitting a portfolio is much the same as in NVQ. It will be prepared according to the guidelines of an approved programme, and will include evidence of competence in teaching, including assessment reports on students, supervision records, videos of sessions, and records of direct observation. The candidate will herself be observed during a supervision session by a practice assessor.

Other post-qualifying training, such as training as an 'approved social worker' in mental health, or in child protection or care management, can attract credits under CCETSW's post-qualification scheme. If the course has been validated by a university or college of higher education, it may also be awarded an academic credit towards a degree under CATS. An agency can develop new units of training to suit its needs, and put them forward for validation. Awards at advanced level can follow the same pattern, but some staff may be sponsored to attend Master's programmes (the agency should make sure that the resulting project or dissertation is relevent to its needs).

8.8   Experience and education

A number of questions arise from the present dominance of competency-based models in social work training:

1. NVQs aren't actually a system of training — merely a system of assessment. Experience + assessment doesn't necessarily add up to learning: there are many things people won't understand unless they are taught, and can't do unless they are trained. In learning from experience, observation depends on having some theory to which you relate what you see. If you are watching say a potter at his wheel you just won't see the skills being used, unless you have been taught something about it first. This applies far more strongly to abstract skills, as in human relations, where a suitable theoretical structure is essential for learning.

2. Experience-learning depends very much on imitation. If your models happen to be outstanding, you may learn a great deal, but if they are mediocre, this sets a ceiling on how far you can progress. NVQs may bring an incompetent performer up to competence, but they have nothing to do with high quality.

3. A common-sense definition of competence is being able to do the job to the satisfaction of consumers, colleagues and superiors. The NVQ definition is 'performing to nationally defined occupational standards', which are now agreed and are available in sheaves of paper. But do the two definitions match up, and what happens if they don't? Is a rigid national curriculum the best way of deciding what staff in a particular location should be able to do?

4. Competence is divided into numerous elements that make up a unit. However interpersonal relations cannot be atomised into a series of stages. A skilled interview is more than the adding together of micro-processes; it depends on empathy, and the ability to convey warmth and genuineness. Social work training is about developing personal qualities and attitudes.

5. The place of understanding and values. The NVQ scheme states clearly that competence is not just about practical skills but also about demonstrating knowledge, understanding, and values (the same combination is required for the Diploma in Social Work, and for post-qualifying training). However it is all very well for NVQ etc. to say that they should be demonstrated, but how are they to be learnt? (Actually they need very different methods as the next section suggests.)

6. There is a danger that intellectual skills will be devalued. Traditional academic education has emphasised conceptual abilities, such as analysis, synthesis, reasoning, hypothesising, and testing evidence, but they may be neglected by concentration on detailed competencies. The aim should be to develop practitioners (at any level) who can think for themselves — take a critical view of current practice and prejudices, be creative and produce new ideas. Competency-based training is bounded by current assumptions.

For these reasons, competency-based training should never stand on its own, but should be placed within a framework of professional development. It should also be supported by off-the-job training, for reasons discussed below.

8.9   Development: the hexagon model

The following sections look in more detail at the processes of development, particularly the development of some of the basic skills and qualities of human behaviour. These qualities are needed in all kinds of work, but they are fundamental to social work where the essence of the job is dealing with people, understanding them and influencing their behaviour. Exactly the same thing is true of managers. In either case, to turn an adequate performer into an excellent one, doesn't mean that they should know more — it means they should behave in a more effective way. The discussion will show why off-the-job training has such an important part in personal development: this does not mean that either the educational or the experience-based approaches are wrong — the three are complementary.

Consider the kind of qualities that distinguish a good social worker — or a good manager, since there will be considerable overlap. Various lists can be found, but most of them include:

Sensitivity
Empathy
Concern
Awareness — of people's reactions, and of other people's lives — e.g. the effects of poverty
Self-organisation
A degree of assertiveness (enough to put forward a case)
Listening
Taking account of others' views
A sense of humour, and proportion
Readiness to learn

How are qualities like these developed? Obviously there are different categories here, which will be developed in different ways: a sense of humour is not the same kind of quality as being self-organised. We first need to clarify what these main categories are. An obvious place to start is with the three kinds of behaviour that are commonly distinguished in psychology — **cognitive, affective** and **active,** or Thinking, Feeling (emotions) and Doing. Each of these has their own sub-classes of behaviour: thinking, for example, includes memorising, classifying, solving problems etc. etc. Effective behaviour is often concerned with the interfaces between these kinds of behaviour — turning an emotional response into a rational one, or moving from thought to action. These interfaces are themselves main classes of behaviour, see Figure 8.1.

- The interface between thinking and doing consists of applying one's brain to practical activities — the area of practical problem solving, learning from experience, and using *skill*.

- The interface between thinking and feeling consists of rationalised emotion — the area of 'attitudes' and 'values'. I both believe that something is so, and feel strongly about it. I dislike councillor Smith because I suspect him to be dishonest: I support the Green party, because its arguments convince me. Attitudes vary from those that are almost wholly rational, to those that are simple prejudice, which we would be hard-pressed to defend intellectually. Values are the fundamental attitudes that make up our outlook on life, particularly our views on right and wrong.

- The interface between doing and feeling consists of the emotions that inspire or accompany action. If I see someone lying injured, and my dominant impulse is to help them, I am showing compassion: if my impulse is to take their wallet, I am showing callousness and greed. In moral philosophy these are called 'virtues', but we are not concerned here with making people virtuous, but making them effective at their job, so it is better to use a less loaded term, such as '**character strengths**'. Some character strengths are obviously needed to be effective in any context — determination, and courage to take risks. But apart from these 'hard' qualities, in social work at least, softer qualities like sympathy and fairness are just as important. Character strengths are closely connected with the 'psychological needs' discussed in chapter 6: for example, determination may often be the result of a strong need for achievement (though the relationship is generally more complex). Although character strengths and values tend to support each other, they are not identical: people can value generosity, but be mean in practice; almost all soldiers admire courage, but not all of them act bravely when the shooting starts.

This sixfold picture of personality is known as the 'hexagon model'.[4]

The qualities of a good social worker listed on p. 152 can be analysed in the light of this model. Listening, empathising, and awareness are *skills*. Self-organisation is mostly a matter of good *practices*, though skills such as planning may underlie it. Concern is a *character strength*, while a sense of humour and of proportion are essentially *values* (acceptance that one's own concerns are not all-important, and that too much solemnity becomes ridiculous). The other qualities are *compound*, in the sense of including two or more elements. Assertiveness is largely a matter of skill (timing one's interventions, judging one's tone of voice) but it also requires some

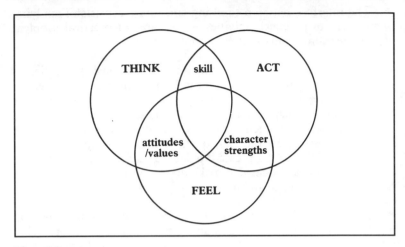

Figure 8.1

courage and determination, and readiness to value one's own contribution. Sensitivity includes both skills (such as awareness and empathising) and values (people's feelings matter). Readiness to learn is an attitude, but ability to learn is an intellectual quality (with elements of skill). This kind of analysis is important, since it shows what development approach is appropriate: you can't teach skill through discussion groups, or character strengths by lectures — they have their own methods of learning, as shown in Table 8.1.

Development of cognitive and active qualities is easier and more acceptable than work with emotions. Psychodynamic training methods such as T Groups have always been suspect, since except with genuine volunteers, they can be a gross invasion of privacy. With young children, we accept the development of character strengths in a way that is essentially behavioural: if they are invariably punished when they steal, they will learn not to, even when the chance of being caught is remote. However with older children and adults, such methods are neither acceptable nor practical, since offenders are not very often caught. The one sound approach to developing character is self-development, which itself depends on acquiring the requisite skill, see below. We are no fonder of the idea that governments should determine people's attitudes. It is all very well to change attitudes through reasoning or new information (in training young people with special needs, there is often a radical change of attitude when they come to see that they have qualities that other people value): however other methods of attitude change, involving pressure and playing on emotions is no business of employers or public authorities. This is not because they don't work — they work only too well, which is why totalitarian regimes continue to flourish.

Table 8.1

Kind of quality	Examples	Methods of development (existing or potential)
Intellectual (thinking skills)	Memorising; creativity; testing theories	School/college curriculum
Skill	Manual skills Professional skills Communication and process skills — planning, listening, reviewing	Training
'Doing': good habits, practices.	Work routines; record-keeping; life routines.	Working under supervision; personal planning; self-discipline.
Character strengths	Courage, determination, concern, generosity, fairness, loyalty	Outward Bound, Guides/Scouts Military training 'Guided self-development'
Feelings Emotional balance	Love, hate — for appropriate objects	Therapy; T Groups
Attitudes Values	Service to community Respect for individuals Equal opportunities	Informed reasoning Indoctrination

Looking again at Figure 8.1, it can be seen that there is a section in the middle where all three circles overlap. This common ground is significant — improvement in one section of the model can benefit the whole personality. A good way to tackle one's emotional problems is to plunge into action: a good way to change attitudes is to develop skill. In a programme of overall development, skill is the best place to start — both because it can be developed fairly readily by training, and because it is an essential ingredient for any form of self-development.

8.10 Kinds of skill[5]

Skills used at work are of two main kinds:

- Technical skills of a task or trade, like typing, driving a vehicle or designing a survey
- Skills of getting things done and communicating with other people. These skills are not specific to any one profession, but can crop up in almost any human activity. They are known as 'process' or 'enabling' skills.

Enabling skills themselves fall into three classes:

- Skills of managing tasks — planning, reviewing, analysing information etc.
- Skills of managing and developing oneself, including planning one's own behaviour, and learning from experience
- Skills of relating to other people. These can be further analysed into:

    (a) Skills of *Transmission* — those concerned with having an impact on others: persuading, informing, leading, restraining, calming down or cheering-up.
    (b) Skills of *Reception* — those concerned with the impact other people have on us: listening, observing, empathising, conforming to someone's mood, or remaining detached.
    (c) *2-Way* Skills: discussing, negotiating, co-operating, sharing out work or building a team.

8.11   Components of skill

Before considering how to develop these skills, we should look briefly at what skill really means. Most skills consist of three elements, which we might call **Awareness**, **Judgement**, and **Dexterity**.

- Awareness is the ability to notice what is going on, and realise that a skilful response is needed.
- Judgement suggests what the response should be;
- Dexterity ensures that the response is made with the necessary finesse and timing.

If I am running a meeting, awareness may tell me that Jane is against my proposal, though she is keeping her objections to herself. Judgement suggests ways of dealing with the problem: in the light of my knowledge of Jane, do I challenge her here and now, or have a quiet word over coffee? Dexterity will ensure that my quiet word is tactful and persuasive. Judgement is based on a set of informal rules that we build up from a lifetime's experience: for dealing with Jane, perhaps a rule such as 'if someone is hostile, talk to them in private, before hostility has a chance to spread'. A rule like this is personal — what works for me: a more extrovert manager might have it out with Jane then and there, and be just as successful. Often these rules are unconscious, though if we pause to review why something we did went well or badly, we may notice the rules we normally follow. Judgement frequently involves a choice between different responses: if Helga is angry, do I get angry back, or apologise and calm her down? The choice may depend on quite complex factors, which if I am making a delayed response — such as answering Helga's letter — I have a chance to think through. But often an immediate response is called for, making judgement the outcome of instinct and experience.

8.12 Developing skill[6]

All skills are developed through a basic cycle of practice and review: try something out, see how it worked, plan to improve, and try again. Review can be strengthened by feedback, from some observer or 'coach' (to use a term from athletics). Sometimes the coach can provide a demonstration, or point out someone's example to imitate. Enabling skills are developed in just this same way: since they are second-order skills — *enabling* you to do something else — there must be some activity on which to practise the skill — a task of some sort. Since the skills to be learnt are interpersonal, the task must involve other people. The cycle of practice and review can take place on the job — which is why it is useful for supervisers to observe trainees in action (provided they take notes, and give detailed feedback). However more concentrated practice can be provided through off-the-job training, structured around tasks and reviews. The task format allows Tackle a Task or some equivalent formula to be practised, in such a way that its use becomes second nature, and the various sub-stages like 'planning' are really understood. On such a course, it is important for trainees to have a chance to act as silent observer, and watch their group in action. This allows them to develop awareness, by seeing how their colleagues operate: and also enables them to give their group some factual feedback in review.

The problem with this sort of training comes from the general nature of the skills. It is easy to provide practice in manual skills, where the actions to be learnt are more or less the same every time. With enabling skills, especially interpersonal skills, useful bits of experience cannot simply be repeated: they have to be broadened into the sort of rules that underlie judgement, and then applied in different contexts. For example, the same principles of persuasion hold true, whether one is dealing with a colleague, a client, or a judge in court: but they have to be adapted for different circumstances. This process of adaptation is known as 'transfer of learning', and has been much studied. Probably the most important finding is that for learning to be actually used, the new 'rules' have to be practised repeatedly, in a range of situations. Training has to ensure that the new skills can be applied again and again in a long sequence of tasks, until they really stick. Another factor in learning is that behaviour changes fast when trainees gain a new perception of themselves, and when people they have come to respect are changing in a similar way. Both these things occur when a training group turns itself into a really strong team. This can be relied on to happen, but only after two or three days. These two factors set a limit on training — to be any use, four or preferably five days are needed. Training of that length can make a profound difference to managers' competence: shorter training gives no benefit at all. This has been the major stumbling block in the spread of these methods: senior management are often prepared to spend money on short courses, but not on longer courses that can convey far more substantial benefits.

Training of the sort described is quite common in management use, provided by various firms of consultants, and has been applied on a large scale by national charities. At the other end of the scale, it has been used quite widely in YTS, including with special needs trainees, with long-term unemployed, and in schools (see below). It has been little used in social work for largely accidental reasons — lack of information leading to lack of demand.

8.13   Self-development

Training in enabling skills is valuable not just for its own sake, but because it can lead on to two other opportunities: self-development, and use of similar methods with clients. Self-development merely needs a brief note, since it arises naturally out of training. The pattern of the course — trial, review and replanning, is the basic method of learning from experience. One of the skills mastered is this basic skill of learning, and people returned from a course can use it deliberately to improve their own performance. As noted above, it is rather difficult to develop character strengths except with volunteers who accept a tough regime. However people who design their own regimes can be as strict as they like. Training courses usually end with a session in which trainees plan some activity for their own future, and young people in particular welcome the opportunity. In an unpublished study of plans made by 100 YTS trainees, nearly all chose some programme of self-improvement as they saw it (stopping smoking, learning to drive, slimming, getting qualified in some way), and of those who were followed up, the majority made progress they saw as satisfactory (one girl wrote 'I have learnt that using this method, I can do anything!). The basic trial–review sequence can easily be adapted to methods based on social learning theory (such as avoiding stimuli for unwanted action): indeed without being taught, many YTS trainees devised methods of this sort for themselves.

8.14   Training and the organisation

(*a*) *Development of teams.*   Successful teamwork depends on of the use of enabling skills, in the context of common aims. Individuals can apply their skills to dealing with their colleagues, and putting their own points across: more usefully, they can apply them to establishing procedures for the team that give everyone the same advantage. If within the team there are people whose aims are strongly opposed, then nothing will get it to work. But if, as is far more usual, basic aims are shared by everyone, then a skilful team can easily cope with the adjustments necessary to make sure that individual aims too are satisfied. The process of training can be a powerful bonding experience, and teams developed in training can be very strong. However where people work together effectively, the same result can be got in daily life.

(*b*) *Organisation development.*   An organisation can be looked on as a network of teams, so common training background can have an equally strong effect on the wider scene. This is particularly important, whereas in so many modern organisations, people move rapidly between several different teams. If people have had the same training, the same procedures can be used throughout, and a group of strangers can be almost as effective as one's own home team. The same approach is used throughout the organisation, and there is usually a vast improvement in communications and morale.

A lot of expertise has been built up in managing organisation-wide training initiatives. It is helpful to start off by training a group of teams who report to the same higher-level boss. It is not necessary to start training at the very top, but fairly senior people (managers of groups of teams) need to be involved early on, and people at the top need at least an informed interest.[7]

8.15   Training and clients

We have noted throughout the book that dealing with clients and
with staff are very similar processes: a professional qualification
doesn't stop one being a human being, and the same hopes, fears and
needs exist, albeit in different strengths. The hexagon model can be
used to show some of the reasons why clients need help — frequently
because of problems in one or more segments. To get the treatment
right, it is crucial to know in which segment the trouble lies — lack
of skill, or faulty values or attitudes, emotional disturbance, defects
of character (lack of kindness or persistence) or simple bad habits.
Of course the problem may lie with a combination of these, but if
one is helped the rest may also improve — in particular there is
nothing like discovering that you had more skills than you supposed
for improving attitudes and habits generally.

Task centred practice is an approach to case work that uses
experience as a way to build-up expertise, morale and the will to
improve. In its use of experience it has something in common with
the NVQ approach to training. What has far less often been tried is
the direct training approach, designed to put across enabling skills.
This is odd, since social workers talk — quite correctly — of
parenting and similar *skills*. Wherever there is a need for a skill there
is a training method that can supply it. Lack of skill should invite a
training response, rather than recourse to child protection procedures.

There have however been some promising trials in using a
training approach. It has been used on quite a large scale in Youth
Training, including schemes for young offenders, and trainees with
learning difficulties or personality disorders.[8] Training programmes
have used the same concepts and sometimes the same tasks as in
training managers and professionals: trainees responded in a very
similar way, groups going through the same stages, and emerging
with very strong morale and enhanced skills. Nearly all trainees were
able to grasp concepts like 'Tackle a Task' quite readily — something some of their own tutors regarded as impossible. As a result
there were marked improvements in the behaviour of trainees, their
ability to co-operate and in relations with staff. Similar training has
been used in primary schools,[9] and once again trainees with learning
difficulties were found to benefit as much as anyone else. Training
has also been used successfully with long-term unemployed adults
(under ET) and as the basis for pre-retirement training. Age does not
seem to make much difference to trainees' responses, at any rate up
to the age of sixty-five: it would be a valuable experiment to try the
approach with still older people.

The essence of training of this sort is empowerment. Trainees discover that they can do more and are effective members of a successful team. As a result their self-esteem is enhanced. Trainees learn to work together for common aims and observe each other's skills. As a result, stereotypes are rapidly falsified, and relations between racial groups quickly improve.[10] There is a tool here crying out to be used.

Notes

1   On NVQ see Harvey, Tisdall, 1992; Kelly, Payne, Warwick 1990.
2   Burton, Dutt, Lyn-Cook 1992.
3   APL is discussed in CCETSW *Credit Accumulation and Transfer in the Diploma in Social Work.*
4   *For the hexagon model, see Taylor, 1990.*
5   *For a taxonomy of skills see Taylor, 1990.*
6   *For the development of skill, see Taylor, Hills 1990.*
7   *For the role of training in organisation development see Taylor, 1992.*
8   *Taylor, Hills 1990.*
9   *Makins, V., Times Educational Supplement 15.12.89.*
10 For example, analysis of a series of mixed groups showed no difference at all between races in the proportion of people who at one time or another took the lead in their group — Taylor 1990. There were however significant differences between the sexes.

9 The management of change

9.1 Effects of changes

Social services are undergoing changes that some people find painful and bewildering. They come not only from new legislation, but from cuts in social service budgets, which will certainly lead to rationing in services, and in some places to enforced redundancy. This is a poor atmosphere for dealing with the changes brought about by legislation. Some people feel that this is all part of one process — the substitution of ideas of profit and the market for gentler, fairer concepts of welfare. Many people see disagreeable consequences for themselves, in terms of new pressures and new skills to master, and strongly suspect that their clients as well as themselves may suffer.

The changes seem all the greater, because the techniques and technology of welfare are so stable. Over the last two hundred years, both the material products of society and the means of making them have been utterly transformed, while the skills of dealing with people have hardly changed at all. A Babylonian scribe coming into a school today would find the processes of education entirely familiar: a conscientious parish priest of Roman or Anglo-Saxon times would have little difficulty in understanding the problems of a social worker. In social work, we can be pretty sure that the same people are going to be administering the same sorts of treatment to the same sorts of client for many years to come. In commerce and industry, firms that are household names may go from prosperity to ruin in a few months, new kinds of job are invented and as quickly disappear, and very few people can count on being in the same career at the age of forty that they chose when they left college. This is not to minimise the changes in social work, but to show that change is pervasive, many people thrive on it, and almost any change provides opportunities as well as difficulties. Over the next few years, social work will be a difficult profession to be in: it will also be like Napoleon's army — a career open to talent.

The biggest immediate changes will come as a result of the contractor–provider split. A good deal of social work will be carried out by independent or semi-independent organisations, largely determining their own policies, setting their own budgets, and responsible for making a profit. There will, as we have seen, be a need for a great deal of new management expertise, and this will provide opportunities for many able people: the opportunities will be not so much those of power — old social service hierarchies gave plenty of scope for controlling other people — but for experiment and achievement: if you have an idea of how social work should be conducted, you have a very good chance of being able to put it into practice — provided you can find a source of funds.

The changes in the core of social service departments will be less striking, but opportunities may be nearly as great. Departments will be smaller, with fewer senior posts, but more chance for relatively junior people to have an impact on policy. The large bureaucratic organisations established after Seebohm may give way to what is being called the 'enabling authority'. Wistow and Knapp[1] suggest three possible interpretations of what this may mean.

Enabling as personal development.   This is central to the philosophy of both the Children Act and community care, and embodies the traditional values of social work. It means working with users and carers on the design of services, and involving them in the assessment of quality.

Enabling as community development.   This means identifying community resources and trying to maintain and extend them. It recognises the strengths of informal support networks and offers help to informal carers. This approach has its roots in the Seebohm and Barclay reports, and builds on the skills and values of community social work.

Enabling as market development.   This involves the development of an independent sector, and active attempts to find alternative ways of meeting needs. The idea is new in social work and has met with both political and professional resistance. However the idea of contracting-out work to the voluntary sector is not new; voluntary agencies have long received grants for carrying out specific pieces of work; children and old people have been paid for in residential homes run by voluntary societies, and adoption work has been contracted-out case by case to adoption societies. The pattern of service provision under contract by charitable or independent organisations is much more common in some European countries, such as Holland. The main political objection is to using private suppliers which 'make a profit out of welfare', though in practice there may be little difference between a company and a charity, since both will plough profits back into the business.

The new organisation may also be 'enabling' in a fourth sense — in the power it gives its own staff to take part in discussions of policy, and control their own working lives. Dealing with social work clients, and dealing with social workers, is part of the same fundamental process of managing people. It requires the same skills, the same knowledge of motivation, and the same ingredients of encouragement, watchfulness and trust — although in different proportions! Moreover the skills that make this possible — the 'enabling' skills discussed in the last chapter, are the same in each case.

How can this come about? As work is contracted to outside providers, social service departments will be smaller, more professional and less monolithic, making it possible to have fewer layers of management between individual operators and the top. The advantages of this are:

- Cost: extra layers of management (and deputies) are not directly productive, and need support staff to service them.
- Communications: every layer of management has to be briefed, which takes time, and can act as a distorting barrier between people at the top and the field.
- A sense of reality — more staff spend some time working in the field.
- Diffusion of power. If team leaders report to people near the top, they can have a direct input into policy.

As a rule of thumb, one manager can control seven or eight direct subordinates (teams can be larger where the pattern of work is stable). By this measure, in the new departments, team leaders should report to a manager only one or at most two levels below the director. (However child care, which will be a larger proportion of the work of the new departments, may be something of a exception to this because of the need for close supervision.)

A lean and healthy organisation will not only have as few as possible levels in the hierarchy, but as few as possible 'experts' at head office. In technological industries, high-placed experts are

essential, since policy depends on their expertise, but in social work
the important policy issues can be understood by almost everyone.
The advantage of shedding specialists is partly a matter of cost, but
still more, of where the director turns to for advice. A director who
has her own advisers on the spot will turn to them first, and only
afterwards to people who run operations in the field. In a healthy
organisation, the people who manage the work also advise on policy,
since they know best what's going on. If team leaders have an impact
on policy, this will increase their status: in private industry (and the
armed services), line jobs reporting to a particular level of management normally outrank staff ones: the factory manager who delivers
the goods is senior to the experts who advise his director. In
government service the opposite is true — people who have an input
on policy rank higher than those who control operations. In central
government there is some reason for this — after all, government
policy affects the whole country, not just the work of civil servants.
However in local government the scope for policy decisions is
actually quite narrow, and it is the way policy is implemented that
really matters. By this yardstick, chief officers are middle rather
than senior managers — concerned with How rather than Why, and
the biggest fault they can commit is to become remote from people
who carry out the work on the ground (the second biggest is to
become remote from their own Council).

If advisers are to be reduced in numbers, where is specialist
advice to come from? The best answer is from the field. In social
work as in most practical subjects, recent experience on the ground
is often more valuable than theory, and task groups drawn from
across the organisation may tackle technical problems better than
specialists. Where specialists exist, they may be better used as
members of devolved teams rather than in head office: a senior social
worker can be part of an area team, and at the same time act as
adviser on her subject to the whole department — chairing a task
group, attending meetings of the Social Services Committee, but
spending three or four days a week on social work. As an example,
the manager of a mental health resources centre remarked that at the
moment she was advising the director — 'if X is away, I am the most
senior person in mental health'. The advantages of a system like this
are cost and immediacy — experts know the problems from current
experience, while individual workers have a chance to serve on task
groups and influence policy.

The main disadvantage is in terms of careers — there will be
fewer senior jobs (one could say 'fewer jobs for the boys', given the
levels of staff affected). A second problem is that a department run
on these lines will need considerable management skills. Senior
people will rely less on power and status, more on consultation and

leadership. Some junior people would have to balance the calls of task groups on which they were serving and their own work-load: Team Leaders would rank higher in the organisation, but have to accept that some of their staff have more expertise in certain areas than they have, and greater impact on policy. They would have to see themselves as links, now heading their own team, now as part of a senior one controlling an important part of the business of the Department. It may hardly matter whether departments are structured by area or by function — whichever system is chosen, there will be a need for liaison groups to work the opposite way round (e.g. if there is a functional split, staff drawn from several departments will have to meet and discuss the problems of communities).

Changes like this are not unique to social work, but in recent years have become common in large and middle-sized organisations. A management consultancy may be based on client groups each controlled by a manager: but individual projects may be staffed by consultants from a mix of teams, and a consultant may find herself in temporary command over her own manager. Managing Directors of technical organisations have long had to accept that engineers, chemists or marketing men know far more about their subjects than they do, and they sometimes have little choice but to follow the lead of their own subordinates. As the American management pundit Rosabeth Moss Kanter writes, 'Some organisations are turning themselves nearly inside out — buying formerly internal services from outside suppliers, forming strategic alliances and supplier–customer partnerships that bring external relationships inside where they can influence policy and practice.' It works — business would not do it otherwise — but it works only when managers make suitable adjustments to their own behaviour. As Kanter goes on to say 'We don't even have good words to describe the new relationships'. 'Superiors' and 'subordinates' hardly seem accurate, and even 'bosses' and 'their people' imply more control and ownership than managers today actually possess.[3]

9.2   Managing change

Managing major change needs the same basic approach as other management tasks, as described in chapters 2 and 6:

- Involving people in discussion from the earliest stage, and doing more listening than talking
- Gathering information about the need for change, and clarifying aims
- Identifying the aims of people affected by change, and seeing that where possible their interests are protected

- Attending to the motivation of people who have to co-operate
- Setting targets tied to a timescale
- Reviewing the means and obstacles to change, the probable consequences (wanted or unwanted), and the risks
- Getting the information, and planning moves in detail
- Selling the change to people not directly involved, and verifying their agreement
- Taking action
- Reviewing the results, in order to plan the next step.

Major change brings in some special considerations:

1. If it is going to affect different sorts of people, manage it through a steering group, on which all the interests are represented. Don't rely on this for communications — make sure that people not involved in it are thoroughly informed, and have a channel for feedback.

2. Know your support. When change is remote, plenty of people will agree, muttering, 'It'll never happen': as action gets nearer, they will begin to drag their feet. Make sure of the attitude of your own bosses: are they really committed, or is their attitude merely acquiescence? If so, whenever the going gets rough they may withdraw their support. You may still choose to go ahead, but judge the risk realistically.

3. Know where the power is, including information, and who can block you. Take steps early to make sure they won't.

4. In any change, there will be winners and losers. Make sure the winners know all about it and are on your side. Identify the losers — including people who fear they will lose, even though you disagree. You may be able to sell the change to them — companies have negotiated changes of work-practice that both sides knew would lead to redundancies. There may be opportunities in the change that you can point out to them. If you can't make change worth losers' while, count on their opposition.

5. Any equilibrium is likely to be held together by a balance of forces. See what holds the present situation static — the pressures for movement, and the pressures for stability or relapse. The pressures may be human but they may equally be technical or financial — the cost of change.

6. Build into your plans whatever is needed to make change stick. Some people who oppose you may let the change happen, reckoning

to kill the baby later when teething problems occur. Often changes depend on people behaving differently: they may do so for a while, and then relapse. How will you get them to stick at it?

7. Above all, if you have a clear vision, let people see it. Someone who clearly knows both the destination, and the way to get there, is the most powerful agent for change.

9.3   Case studies in the management of change

Here are three case studies of the management of change. The first is of a new small-scale voluntary organisation, aiming to provide a specialist service for local authorities.

The Adolescent and Children's Trust (TACT)

The Adolescent and Children's Trust is an example of a new breed of voluntary organisation, which takes account of the contract culture and the increasing demand for quality assurance. It was born out of the provisions of the 1989 Children Act to provide specialist foster care placements for a whole range of children in need, from those who are disabled to sexually abused adolescents. It is set up and run by a small group of social work professionals, who are also professional managers. TACT earns its own living through fees paid by local authorities for the foster care services provided. As a voluntary organisation and registered charity, governed by a Council of Management, all activities are closely scrutinised and surplus revenue is fed back into new projects for children. The Council of Management have no financial interest in the organisation.

The organisation has developed through a number of changes. It started in 1986 with one freelance consultant, who originally offered local authorities a range of services, including training, professional auditing, and consultancy for development projects. The move into fostering services came in 1988, when a local authority asked for help in placing an adolescent. The young person was successfully placed and the Project Director realised that there was a demand from local authorities for foster care placements. The first mailshot met with an instant response: the leaflet went out on Friday and on Monday there was an invitation to meet with a local authority, who soon signed a contract for emergency placements. Over the next 18 months, work snowballed and it was necessary to increase the staff and form a limited company. A key turning point was the preparation of the first business plan; drawn up with professional advice in order to gain co-operation from the bank. As with any small business a problem particularly in these early days was cash flow; the foster carers had to be paid on a weekly basis, but local authorities paid in arrears, and often after delay.

In 1990 a second member of professional staff and an administrator joined the team. The next year was a period of preparation and planning for the implementation of the Children Act and for the application for Trust status. The reasons for the change to charitable status were two-fold. First, the shared use of foster carers between agencies was cumbersome and would become more so under the new regulations. Secondly, the organisation wished to work closely in partnership with local authorities, and considered that it was politically preferable to do so on a 'not-for-profit' basis. In order to make an application to the Charity Commissioners it was necessary to appoint a group of trustees. A fostering panel was set up, and fresh publicity and marketing material were produced. All of this involved clarifying and agreeing a professional philosophy and in particular, emphasis was placed on the following points:

— The ability to approach and deal with senior local authority staff as fellow professionals with shared experience and skills;
— Simply but effectively produced 'sales' literature setting out TACT's philosophy of child care alongside a detailed explanation of the services offered;
— Quality assurance in the form of:
  direct operational scrutiny by the Council of Management;
  the use of independent professionals to assess and review TACT's foster carers;
  regular review meetings with local authorities;
  a fostering panel which is multi-disciplinary and independently based;
  a clearly documented and well-circulated complaints procedure;
  seeking registration for BS 5750
— Individually designed training programmes for all TACT foster carers, which will in the future be linked to NVQ
— an equal opportunity policy which has been implemented in the composition of the fostering panel and the foster carers considered for approval. Over 50 per cent of the approved foster carers are black.

On the management side, TACT continues to operate as a small co-operative team with a core management group of five, who are responsible for professional standards, training and recruitment, marketing, and link work. Beyond this is a network of consultants, who are employed on a short-term basis for particular projects, and each of whom reports to a member of the core group and attends meetings as needed. Much work is done from home so that the costs of office accommodation are kept to a minimum, and communication is maintained by telephone and bleep, with the administrator as the linchpin. A key concern continues to be the analysis of gaps in the market in order to find viable new projects. The director continues to have the role of researching new possibilities, but now with a strong team structure, he brings back proposals for discussion and decision on viability. Any idea proposed should reflect the ethos of the agency, and so there is attention to putting up high-quality ideas rather than following every available possibility. With the move to more contracting-out, the organisation is faced with the problems of success; how far to expand and in what directions, without losing the impetus of the work already done?

★   ★   ★

The second case study is a new medium-sized voluntary organisation, set up to run a resource previously administered by a public body.

Opportunities and Networks in Southwark (ONIS)

ONIS provides services for people with learning difficulties; the organisation now has 40 members of staff. This brief case-study cannot draw on all of the feelings shared by the managers in the interview. Their account of the initial stages of the project had a sense of energy and excitement, coupled with memories of overload, brought about by taking on so many new things, and having to do everything at once.

In 1990 the Health Authority encouraged Southwark Consortium to become a managing agency, and at the same time hived off parts of its own organisation as not-for-profit units. ONIS was set up in 1990 to operate as a separate organisation, in order to pilot the contractual relationship with individual service agreements. This gave a lead-in period of 18 months before the application for company status in April 1992. For the two managers appointed to the project, there was a steep learning curve in the first year; they had to learn about finance and company law, and decide on what sort of company structure was needed; they needed financial information, which the Health Authority wasn't always able to provide because the existing systems could not break the budget down in detail. They found that the relationship with their former line manager changed, and although he continued to be supportive, the relationship was now contractual.

The process of negotiating individual service agreements for each client led to a radical review of the nature of the service. The initial aim when people left hospital had been to create a perfect supported housing scheme, and this had meant that the scheme itself rather than the individual had become the aim of the service. Individuals needed much more independence and ways of integrating into the community. In the initial stages of negotiating service agreements, the managers kept coming back to each other and saying, 'this person's service isn't right', and they found that overall the service wasn't reflecting the needs and wants of the users. Many people were over-supported and they had to try to think of alternatives; some people were provided with a cocoon of staff and were given 24-hour support a day, so that the staff met all their needs and they had no need to seek social links; they were using the staff as friends, but professionals can't be friends.

If the aims of the service were to change, the structure of the organisation had to change. At first there were five addresses and the staff were attached to the address; this led to them providing support to the houses rather than the people in them. The managers therefore decided to change to four staff teams with each staff member responsible for a number of clients, and the teams divided by skills rather than geography, for example work with elderly clients, or those with challenging behaviour. Thus the teams are built around client needs, and the role of the staff shifted from support worker to co-ordinator, facilitating a number of different inputs from volunteers, home helps, cleaners, advocates and voluntary groups. Some clients, of course, will still need intensive support, sometimes up to 24-hours a day, but support of that kind requires overwhelming amounts of staff; so one must always ask whether it is really necessary.

In order to change the staffing structure, posts were left vacant as they occurred. They wished to re-organise in order to provide posts for project leaders. A project leader has a role which is split 60/40 between development and management, with 60 per cent of time allocated to development. This definite allocation of time for development arose from the experience of the two managers, who suffered from overload in the first year, because although one post had a development brief, this included the development of five other organisations.

During the pilot year the managers spent a great deal of time working with staff in order to gain their support for the changes. Support workers, who had previously worked for the health authority, did not see themselves as part of an organisation; they felt detached and isolated, with little contact with the health authority, which was seen as impersonal and monolithic. Now they have a strong sense of belonging to an organisation. This was built up in the first year by going to meetings on a regular basis, once every six weeks to each team. The managers prepared a questionnaire about fears and expectations, and asked staff to fill it in, anonymously, but stating their team. On the basis of this it was possible to gear the meetings to the particular concerns of staff. They then prepared an initial statement on the culture of the organisation and had two consultation sessions, for which all staff were given agency cover. The statement was discussed in mixed staff groups and the day ended with a very successful social event.

It was important at first to get the right people into key posts, especially the administrator, and to get the right financial systems. The first business plan was produced to satisfy the bank manager, but the current plan draws together a financial plan with a plan for service delivery. Each project leader has aims and objectives for the year, and aims are worked out for each team leader and support worker; this then forms the basis of performance review. The plan is essential for marketing with the commissioning agency, but is also used more widely in order to spread good practice. The service has moved away from responding to crisis to providing a planned service, but they are still willing to take risks and go for innovations, for example in renting a property for a particular client, or in abolishing sleep in cover, or in developing shared living arrangements. Looking back, some of the key points have been the need for support for the managers themselves (which is now provided by the Chair of the Board), the advantages of having paired managers rather than one alone, and the importance of designated time for development work.

The third case study is a large social services department, which intends to continue as a provider of services but has moved to a devolved structure with delegated budgets and published quality standards.

Lewisham Social Services

Lewisham has developed quality standards for all its front line service units. The history of this development goes back to 1987, when the mission statement and core values were introduced for all the Council's services as part of a public services orientation. In 1988 each department of the Council was asked to develop a service programme and targets for each service area, and there was the beginning of a programme of devolved management, for housing neighbourhood offices and service achievement centres (SACS), with devolved budgets, in environmental services. In 1991 Social Services established six service achievement centres in selected services. A departmental policy review began in the summer of 1991, and recommended a department-wide devolution in January 1992. The objectives of the devolved structure were increased account-ability, a new and more 'business-like' approach, and a clear and positive structure. The department has now been devolved into 60 service units under eight heads of service; four professional advisers report to the heads of service. They have no line management responsibility, but will act as consultants on professional practice.

Each service unit is asked, in response to a service brief, to develop a service plan. The plan includes:

— demography, legislation and current policy
— philosophy and service aims, with reference to current com-mittee policy
— changes in strategy and issues to be addressed with indicators and targets
— a review of the past year, and plans for the coming year
— a service delivery statement for users
— a budget
— quality standards.

From April 1993 each service unit manager will negotiate the plan with the management board, in order to arrive at a cash-limited budget, which will include salary costs. Each unit has developed and published quality standards, and the process has enabled the units to arrive at important benchmarks for themselves. As these have been the result of consultation and staff discussion, they are very varied; some units have developed detailed flow-charts and performance indicators, while for others standards are more generalised. Through publication, comment is invited, so that standards can be revised and reviewed as need be.

Some key points in the process of change have been:

1. Development sessions for service unit managers have pro-vided training and also a lateral support network, so that problems and issues are shared across settings.
2. A designated post of change agent co-ordinator with a short-term development brief.
3. Active backing by the Chair, the Director and the Chief Executive.
4. Publicity and public relations material, including a sup-plement to the Council's newspaper for residents, and a seminar

for other professionals on quality standards, to which service unit managers made presentations.

5. A recognition that people respond to change at a different pace, and that those who are slow to come round can be won over, once they see what others are doing and catch a sense of enthusiasm.

6. Honesty in sharing problems.

One spin-off of the development process has been the networking of ideas and resources between managers. Among these are the successful bid for joint finance for a mental health support worker for the deaf (this had started as a pilot project in one day centre with hours bought in from deaf people to act as support workers); a plan to pursue European finance to provide a range of services and facilities at a day centre for people with disabilities; a partnership with a local housing association to set up an independent living scheme, with finance from the Housing corporation to buy the property, and joint finance to employ a support worker; a successful bid for joint finance for an interpreter post in sign language; and the provision of a rest room at a children's resource centre.

9.4   Discussion of the case studies

A number of general themes can be identified:

1. Each organisation has in different ways used the current changes to draw up or to clarify its aims and philosophy. For TACT this work was part of the preparation of the brochure, and the application for charity status. At ONIS the work on aims went through a number of stages, from the preparation of an outline document on the culture of the organisation to the preparation of the current business plan. For Lewisham, as for many other social services departments, there have been different levels of policy development, from the initial agreement of a council-wide mission statement and core values to detailed service plans for individual units.

2. Concentration on aims has gone hand in hand with budgeting. For the two voluntary organisations, preparing a business plan has been a key task. In the social services department, the service plan is just as important. But as ONIS found, the shift from public finance to private budgeting is not an easy one, largely because public services have not, up to now, been costed in detail.

3. Change was brought about through a process of consultation. This is most evident in ONIS, where staff were faced with a change of employer as well as a change of task, role and organisation structure. The managers' response was a programme of staff consultation, combined with strategic decisions about necessary changes.

4. Linked to this is a clear recognition of the need for designated development time. This is met in different ways: at ONIS through posts which are partly or entirely designated for development; at Lewisham through the creation of a temporary development post; and at TACT partly through the continuing role of the director, but also through the use of consultants to undertake specific development projects, such as the preparation of the agency to apply for BS 5750.

5. Quality standards are emphasised in each organisation: Lewisham is using published quality standards in a major drive for public accountability; TACT are in the process of putting together an application for BS 5750, and see the maintenance of professional standards as essential; ONIS also see quality standards as a way of promoting new ways of working.

6. For the voluntary organisations marketing is of central importance. For TACT, with no established history or pre-existing client group, marketing was an imperative, but the organisation is quite clear that the search for new business must be combined with high professional standards. ONIS inherited a client group, and has added an additional contract, so that the organisation is now seen as being at optimum size; marketing therefore is as much concerned with professional issues as with gaining new clients. For Lewisham, as for most social services departments, marketing is about public credibility and political accountability: to thrive in the new climate social services must demonstrate both.

7. Finally all three organisations have a structure which allows primary loyalty to a small group, but in different ways allow for cross-fertilisation and the generation of new ideas through networks of support.

These are the themes that have been the focus of this book. Anyone currently involved in social work will recognise them and be able to think of other organisations which demonstrate the same approach, though of course there will be infinite variations. We have sought to explore some of the possibilities of the new way of doing things. However, this is not to discount some of the drawbacks;

innovation is only possible if is supported by adequate funds, and unlikely in an atmosphere of drastic cutback; quality standards depend on checking and inspection, and inspection units vary considerably in their ability to do this job; many needs will continue to be 'unmet' and may never be carried forward into future plans. How the reforms are implemented in each area will depend on how services have developed locally, on the strength of the voluntary sector, and the political views of the Council. The new world of social work will look different from the old: whether it gives clients a better deal will depend on the skills of managers.

Notes

1   Wistow, G., Knapp, M., Hardy, P., Allen, C. (1992) 'From providing to enabling: local authorities and the mixed economy of care'. *Public Administration* **70** Spring p.24 ff.
2   Kanter, R.M. (1989) 'The new managerial work'. *Harvard Business Review* November/December pp. 85–92.

Bibliography

Abernathy, W.J., Clark K.B., Kantrow A.M. (1983) *Industrial Renaissance*. New York: Basic Books.

Adair, J. (1983) *Effective Leadership*. London: Gower.

Ahmad, B. (1991) *Equal Opportunity Training: a guide for practice*. London Race Equality Unit/NISW.

Ahmad, B. (1990) *Black Perspectives in Social Work*. London: Venture Press.

Ahmad, B. (1992) *Dictionary of Black Managers in White Organisations*. London: Race Equality Unit/NISW.

Ajzen, I., Fishbein M., (1980) *Understanding Attitudes and Predicting Social Behaviour*. Eaglewood Cliffs: Prentice-Hall.

Allen, I. (1990) *Care Managers and Care Management*. London: Policy Studies Institute.

Allen, I. Hogg, D. Peace, S. (1992) *Elderly People: choice participation and satisfaction*. London: Policy Studies Institute.

Anscombe, G.E.M. (1954) *Intention*. Oxford: Oxford University Press.

Argyll, M. (1983) *The Psychology of Interpersonal Behaviour*, 4th ed. Harmondsworth: Penguin.

Aristotle, *Ethics* (Nicomachean ethics), translated by Rackham, H. (1934). London/ Harvard: Loeb.

Association of Directors of Social Services/Commission for Racial Equality (1976) *Multi-racial Britain: the social services response* London: CRE.

Association of Metropolitan Authorities (1991) *Contracts for Care*. London: AMA.

Atkinson, J.W., Birch, D. (1976) *An Introduction to Motivation*. New York London: D. Van Nostrand.

Audit Commission (1986) *Making a Reality of Community Care*. London: HMSO.

Bandura, A. (1977) *Social Learning Theory*. New Jersey: Prentice Hall.

Beardshaw, V., Towell, D. (1990) *Assessment and Case Management*. Briefing Paper No. 10. London: Kings Fund.

Beckhard, R. (1969) *Organisation Development, Strategies and Models*. London: Addison-Wesley.

Bennis, W.G. (1969) *Organisation Development, Its Nature, Origins and Prospects*. London: Addison-Wesley.

Belbin, R.M. (1981) *Management Teams: why they succeed or fail*. London: Heinemann.

Berry, J., Jones, B. (1988) *Whose Social Services?* London; Association of Metropolitan Authorities.

Biggs, S., Weinstein, J. (1991) *Assessment and Care Management and Inspection in Community Care.* London CCETSW.

Blagg, H., Smith, D. (1989) *Crime, Penal Policy and Social Work.* Harlow: Longman.

Burns, J.M. (1978) *Leadership.* New York: Harper and Row.

Burton, S., Dutt, R., Lyn-Cook, S., (1992) *Black Perspectives in S/NVQ.* London Race Equality Unit/NISW.

Butt, J., Gorbach, P., Ahmad, B. (1991) *Equally Fair?* London: Race Equality Unit/NISW.

Cassam, E. Gupta, H. (1992) *Quality Assurance for Social Care Agencies.* Harlow: Longman.

Centre for Policy on Ageing (1988) *Home Life.*

Challis, D. Darton, R., Johnson, L., Stone, M., Traske, K., Wall, B. (1989) *Darlington Community Care Project; supporting frail elderly people at home.* Canterbury: University of Kent PSSRU.

Challis, D., Chesum, R., Chesterman, R., Luckett, T., Traske, K. (1990) *The Gateshead Community Care Scheme: case management in social and health care.* Canterbury. University of Kent PSSRU.

Challis, L., Fuller, S., Henwood, M., Klein, R., Plowden, W., Webb, A., Whittingham, P., Wistow, G., (1988) *Joint Approaches to Social Policy.* Cambridge: Cambridge University Press.

Checkland, P. (1981) *Systems Thinking and Systems Practice.* Chichester: Wiley.

Checkland P. and Scholes J. (1990) *Soft Systems Methodology in Action.* Chichester: Wiley.

Cheetham, J., Fuller, R., McIvor, G., Petch, A. (1992) *Evaluating Social Work Effectiveness.* Buckingham: Open University Press.

Connelly, N. (1988) *Caring in a Multiracial Community.* London: Policy Studies Institute.

Commission for Racial Equality (1989) *Racial Equality in Social Services Departments: a survey of equal opportunity policies.* London CRE.

Common, R., Flynn, N. (1992) *Contracting for Care.* York: Joseph Rowntree.

Coulshed, V. (1990) *Management in Social Work.* London: Macmillan.

Craighead, W.E., Kazdin, A.E., Mahoney, M.J. (1976) *Behaviour Modification: principles, issues and applications.* Boston: Houghton Mifflin.

Croft, S., Beresford, P. (1990) *From Paternalism to Participation; involving people in social services.* London: Open Services Project/Joseph Rowntree.

Curnock, K., Hardiker, P. (1979) *Towards Practice Theory: skills and methods in social assessment.* London: Routledge & Kegan Paul.

Darvill, G., Smale, G. (1990) *Partners in Empowerment: networks of innovation in social work.* London: National Institute of Social Work.

Davis, A., Mansell, C. and P., Winner, M. (1992) *Exploring Competence in Registration, Inspection and Quality Control.* London: CCETSW.

Department of Health (1989) *Caring for People: Community Care in the next decade and beyond.* London: HMSO.

Department of Health (1989) *Principles and Practice in Regulations and Guidance.* London.

Department of Health (1990) *Child Care Policy: putting it in writing.* London: HMSO.

Department of Health (1990) *Management Development: guidance for local authority Social Services Departments.* London: HMSO.

Department of Health (1991) *Inspecting for Quality.* London: HMSO.

Department of Health (1991) *The Right of Service.* London: HMSO.

Department of Health (1991) *The Purchase of Service.* London: HMSO.

Department of Health (1991) *Working Together under the Children Act 1989.* London: HMSO.

Department of Health and Social Services Inspectorate (1991) *Purchasing Commissioning and Provider Roles.* London: HMSO.

Department of Health (1992) *Children Act Report 1992.* London: HMSO.

Department of Health (1992) *Promoting Women: management development and training for women in social services.* London: HMSO.

Department of Health (1992) *Quality Assurance in Social Services Departments.* London: HMSO.

Doel, M., Marsh, P. (1992) *Task-Centred Social Work.* Aldershot: Ashgate.

Doyal, L., Gough, I. (1991) *A Theory of Human Need.* London: Macmillan.

Dutfield, M. (1993) *Effective Contract Management.* Birmingham: PEPAR.

Drucker, P.F. (1954) *The Practice of Management.* New York: Harper and Row.

Drucker, P.F. (1985) *Innovation and Entrepreneurship.* New York: Harper and Row.

Ellis, H.C. (1965) *The Transfer of Learning.* New York: Macmillan.

Ellis, K. (1993) *Squaring the Circle: user and carer participation in needs assessment.* York: Joseph Rowntree.

Fishbein, M. and Ajzen, I. (1975) *Belief, Attitude, Intention and Behaviour: an introduction to theory and research.* Reading Mass: Addison-Wesley.

Fisher and Ury (1982) *Getting to Yes, Negotiating Without Giving In.* London: Hutchinson.

Fisher, M., (1983) *Speaking of Clients.* Sheffield: Joint Unit for Social Services Research.

Flynn, N. (1990) *Public Sector Management.* Hemel Hempstead: Harvester Wheatsheaf.

Gagné, R.M. (1977) *The Conditions of Learning* 3rd ed. New York: Holt, Rinehart and Winston.

Gaitley, R., Seed, P. (1989) *HIV and AIDs: a social network approach.* London: Jesica Kingsley.

Gilbert, P., Scragg, T. (1992) *Managing to Care: the management of services for people with learning difficulties.* Sutton: Community Care/Reed.

Glampson, A., Scott, T. (1975) *A Guide to the Assessment of Community Needs and Resources.* London: NISW.

Goldberg, E., Warburton, R. (1979) *Ends and Means in Social Work.* London: George Allen and Unwin.

Griffiths, R. (1992) 'With the past behind us' *Community Care* January 16 p.18–21.

Grimwood, C. Popplestone, R. (1993) *Women in Management and Care.* London: Macmillan.

Hallett, C. (1989) *Women and Social Service Departments.* Hemel Hempstead: Harvester Wheatsheaf.

Hallett, C., Birchall, E. (1992) *Coordination and Child Protection: a review of the literature.* London: HMSO.

Hamblin, A.C. (1974) *Evaluation and Control of Training.* London: McGraw-Hill.

Harris, G.G. (1973) 'The use of modelling procedures' *Journal of Community Psychology,* **1**, 298–301.

Harvey, M., Tisdall, C. (1992) *Vocational Qualifications for Care.* Birmingham: PEPAR.

Harvey-Jones, J. (1988) *Making it Happen, Reflections on Leadership.* London: Collins.

Hawkley, K. (1992) *From Grants to Contracts: a practical guide for voluntary organisations.* London: NCVO.

Hayes, R., Clark, K.B., Wheelwright, S. (1988) *Dynamic Manufacturing: creating the learning organisation.* New York: Free Press.

Hearn, B., Darvill, G., Morris, P., (1992) *On Becoming a Manager,* Harlow: Longman.

Hilgard, E.R., Atkinson, R.C., Atkinson, R.L. (1975) *Introduction to Psychology,* 6th ed. San Diego; London: Harcourt Brace Jovanovich.

Hood, C. (1991) 'A public management for all seasons?' *Public Administration* Spring 1991, **69** pp.3–19.

Hunter, D. (1993) 'To market! To market! A new dawn for community care'. *Health and Social Care in the Community* Vol. 1 No. 1 January 1993 pp.3–10.

Jeffs, T., Smith, M. (ed.) (1987) *Youth work*. Basingstoke: Macmillan Education.

Jesness, C.F. (1975) 'Comparative effectiveness of behaviour modification and transactional analysis programmes for delinquents' *Journal of Consulting and Clinical Psychology*, **43**, 758–79.

Kanter, R.M. (1972) *Commitment and Community*. Cambridge, Mass: Harvard University Press.

Kanter, R.M. (1989) 'The new managerial work' *Harvard Business Review* November/December 1989 pp.85–92.

Kelly, D., Warr, B. (1992) *Quality Counts*. Whiting and Birch.

Kelly, D., Payne, C., Warwick, J. (1990) *Making Vocational Qualifictions Work in Social Care*. London: NISW.

Knapp, M., Cambridge, P., Thomason, C., Beecham, J., Allen, C., Darton, R. (1992) *Care in the Community; Challenge and Demonstration*. Aldershot: Ashgate.

Lawrie, A. (1992) *Quality of Service*. London: NCVO.

Lefcourt, H.M. (1976) *Locus of Control: current trends in theory and research*. New York; London: Wiley.

Likert, R. (1967) *The Human Organisation*. New York: McGraw-Hill.

McClelland, D.C. (1962) *The Achieving Society*. Princeton NJ: Van Nostrand.

McClelland, D.C. (1975) *Power, the Inner Experience*. New York: Wiley.

McClelland, D.C., Atkinson, J.W., Clarke, R.A. and Lowell, E.L. (1953) *The Achievement Motive*. New York: Appleton-Century-Crofts.

McClelland, D.C., Winter, D. (1969) *Motivating Economic Achievement*. New York: The Free Press.

McGregor, D. (1960) *The Human Side of Enterprise*. New York: McGraw-Hill.

Mahoney, M.J., Thoresen, C.E. (1974) *Self-control: power to the person*. Belmont, Calif: Brooks-Cole.

Marsh, P., Fisher, M. (1992) *Good Intentions: developing partnership in Social Services*. York: Joseph Rowntree.

Matheson, J. *Voluntary Work: a study carried out as part of the 1987 General Household Survey*. London: Office of Population, Census and Surveys. HMSO.

Meadows, A. (1992) *Reaching Agreement: Wiltshire's experience of service agreements*. London: NCVO.

Miller, C., Crosbie, D., Vickery, A. (1991) *Everyday Community Care: a manual for managers*. London: National Institute of Social work.

Mischel, W. (1973) 'Towards a cognitive social learning conceptualisation of personality'. *Psychological Review*, pp.252 ff.

Murray, H.A. (1938) *Explorations in Personality; a clinical and experiential study of 50 men of college age by the workers of Harvard Psychology Clinic*. New York: OUP.

National Consumer Council (1992) *Getting Heard and Getting Things Changed*. London: NCC.

National Institute of Social Work (1988) *Residential Care: a positive choice*. Report of the Independent Review of Residential Care chaired by Gillian Wagner. London: HMSO.

Netten, A., Becham, J. (1993) *Costing Community Care: theory and practice*. Aldershot: Ashgate.

Osborne, S. (1991) 'The Management of Need: the role of case management and the allocation of community care resources' *Local Government Studies* January/February pp.5–12.

Osborne, S. (1992) 'The quality dimension in human services' *British Journal of Social Work* Vol. 22 No. 4 August pp.437 ff.

Oynett, S. (1990) *Case Management in Mental Health*. London: Chapman and Hall.

Packman, J., Randall, J., Jacques, N. (1986) *Who Needs Care? Social Work Decisions in Child Care*. London: Blackwell.

Parsloe, P. (1981) *Social Service Area Teams*. London: George Allen and Unwin.

Patel, N. (1990) *A Race Against Time: social service provision for black elders*. London: Runnymede Trust.

Payne, C., Scott, T. (1982) *Developing Supervision of Teams in Field and Residential Work*. London: NISW.

Percy-Smith, J., Saderson, I. (1992) *Understanding Local Needs*. London: Institute for Public Policy Research.

Perrow, C. (1970) *Organisational Analysis: a sociological view*. London: Tavistock.

Peters, T.J. (1987) *Thriving on chaos*. New York: Alfred A. Knopf.

Plant, R. (1987) *Managing Change and Making it Stick*. London: Fontana.

Rao, N. (1992) *From Providing to Enabling: local authorities and community care*. York: Joseph Rowntree.

Rees, S., Wallace, A. (1982) *Verdicts on Social Work*. London; Edward Arnold.

Renshaw, J., Hampson, R., Thomason, C., Darton, R., Judge, K., Knapp, M. (1988) *Care in the Community: the first steps*. Aldershot: Gower.

Richards, M., Payne, C., Sheppard, A. (1990) *Staff Supervision in Child Protection Work*. London: NISW.

Ross, S., Bilson, A. (1989) *Social Work Management and Practice*. London: Jessica Kingsley.

Ryburn, M. (1991): 'The Children Act: power and empowerment' *Adoption and Fostering* Vol. 15 no. 3. p.10.

Schein, E.H. (1969) *Process Consultation: its role in organisational development*. London: Addison-Wesley.

Singer, E.J. (1974) *Effective Management Coaching*. London: Institute of Personnel Management.

Simons, K. (1992) *'Sticking Up for Yourself': self advocacy and people with learning difficulties*. York: Joseph Rowntree.

Smith, P.B. (1973) *Groups within Organisations*. London: Harper and Row.

Stevenson, O. (1981) *Specialisation in Social Service Teams*. London: George Allen and Unwin.

Stevenson, O., Parsloe, P. *Community Care and Empowerment*. York: Joseph Rowntree.

Stewart, A., Stewart, V. (1981) *Tomorrow's Managers Today* 2nd ed. London: Institute of Personnel Management.

Taylor, M. (1992) *Coverdale on Management* 2nd ed. Oxford: Butterworth-Heinemann.

Taylor, M. (1985) *Getting Things Done*. London: FEU.

Taylor, M. (1990) *Effectiveness in Education and Training*. Aldershot: Gower.

Taylor, M., Hills, S. (1990) *Training for Special Needs*. Harlow: Longman.

Thoresen, C.E. and Mahoney, M.J. (1974) *Behavioural Self-control*. Holt Rinehart and Winston.

Thorpe, D.H., Smith, D., Green, C.J., Paley J.H. (1980) Out of Care: the community support of juvenile offenders. London: George Allen and Unwin.

Veiga, J.F. and Yanouzas, J.N. (1979) *The Dynamics of Organization Theory*. St Paul: West Publishing Co.

Walsh, K. (1991) 'Quality and public services' *Public Administration* Vol. 69 Winter 1991 p.503 ff.

Webb, A. (1991) 'Coordination: a problem in public sector management' *Policy and Politics* Vol. 19 no. 4 pp.229–41.

Windle, K., Kerslak, A., Wright, I., Berry, S. (1992) *Capital Care Management*. SSRADU University of Bath.

Wistow, G., Knapp, M., Hardy, B., Allen, C. (1992) 'From providing to enabling: local authorities and the mixed economy of care' *Public Administration* Vol. 70 Spring pp.25 ff.